LISBON

By the staff of Editions Berlitz

Berlitz Trademark Reg. U.S. Patent Office and other countries –
Marca Registrada. Library of Congress Catalog Card No. 78-70374.
Printed in Switzerland by Weber SA, Bienne.

Updated edition 1981

Preface

A new kind of travel guide for the jet age—and one of an extensive series by Berlitz on the world's top tourist areas—this compact and colourful book is packed with all you need to know about Lisbon.

Like our phrase books and dictionaries, this book fits your pocket—in both size and price. It also aims to fit your travel needs:

- It concentrates on your specific destination—Lisbon—not an entire country.

- It combines easy reading with fast facts: what to see and do, where to shop, what to eat.

- An authoritative A-to-Z "blueprint" fills the back of the book, giving clear-cut answers to all your questions, from "What number do I call if my car breaks down?" to "Where can I change money on the weekends?"—plus how to get there, when to go and what to budget.

- Easy-to-read maps in full colour pinpoint sights you'll want to see and provide handy reference for visiting the city and surrounding scenic regions.

Let your travel agent help you choose a hotel. Let a restaurant guide help you choose a good place to eat. But to decide "What should we do today?" travel with Berlitz.

Area specialist: Ken Bernstein
Photography: Dany Gignoux
Design: Doris Haldemann
We wish to thank the Portuguese National Tourist Office in Geneva, particularly Luis Rocha, for much valuable assistance in the preparation of this book.
ⓕ Cartography: Falk-Verlag, Hamburg.

How to use this guide
If time is short, look for items to visit which are printed in bold type in this book, e.g. **Estufa Fria.** Those sights most highly recommended are not only given in bold type but also carry our traveller symbol, e.g. **Mosteiro dos Jerónimos.**

Contents

Maps: Lisbon—Centre p. 24–25, Alfama p. 38, Belém p. 42, Estoril Coast p. 62, Excursions p. 73. *Photo* (p. 2–3): Praça do Comércio.

The City
and the People

In an uncompromising world of extremes, Lisbon steers for the happy medium. Don't expect to be shown the world's widest plaza or tallest cathedral. Extravagant claims are few. Most superlatives are in the people themselves—the kindest and most dignified you're likely to meet. And the most modest.

With a keen eye for beauty, they decorate their balconies with flower pots, the walls with patterned tiles, the sidewalks with mosaics. Old women in black take their brightly decorated bread bags to the bakery to be filled with oven-warm rolls. Any neighbourhood park keeps a few swans or ducks as pets; in the bigger ones peacocks squat in the trees or strut across your path. But do save some film for the wide-angle sights. This is a city of hills and

vantage-points—not seven hills as legend claims, but nearly two dozen. Each gives a new perspective over the tile roofs and the magnificent harbour.

Here the Tagus River, nearing the end of a long journey from the mountains of eastern Spain, swells into what's called the Straw Sea. (The name is poetical, not literal; the sun casts golden, straw-like reflections on the wide waters.) Passing Lisbon the river narrows sufficiently to be spanned by one of those rare local superlatives, Europe's longest suspension bridge. And then the Tagus flows to meet the ocean, as the daring explorers did when they sailed from Lisbon in the 15th and 16th centuries to found the farthest-flung empire of the age.

Although the Atlantic begins

Shady lookout point surveys roofs of Alfama, where dark-eyed fado singers wail their nostalgic songs.

only a few miles down the estuary, the climate is strictly Mediterranean. Palm trees and bird-of-paradise flowers flourish in the mild winters. The balmy weather encourages an unhurried pace in this capital of nearly a million inhabitants. There's always time enough to pause for a cup of coffee or a breath of clean air. The most conspicuous local industries—shipbuilding, commerce and government—don't have polluting smokestacks.

Though the history of Lisbon goes back at least 3,000 years, the range of ancient monuments is limited. Among other reasons, a cataclysmic earthquake crumbled many fine churches and palaces in 1755. The notable survivor is the Castle of St. George at the top of Lisbon's highest hill, begun by the Visigoths and expanded by the Moors. As you walk its forbidding battlements you can appreciate the determination of the crusaders who captured it after a four-month siege in 1147. The ramparts, whose outlines are now softened by moss and ivy, protect a lovely park inhabited by pink flamingos, black ravens and white deer.

Almost everywhere you'll see evidence—mostly circumstantial—of Lisbon's distant past: the Phoenician profile of the modern fishing boats, the Moorish expertise with painted tiles, the sad dark eyes of the people. Listen to their music, the *fado*, and ponder the timeless cry of longing and lament.

The *fado* is most at home in Lisbon's oldest neighbourhood, Alfama. Not only are there nightclubs specializing in this folklore attraction, you can hear it any day as you explore the steep winding streets. Listen to the melodic plaint escaping through the windows of medieval tenements. The saddest of songs may come from a radio or record player, or spontaneously in the voices of the local women and children. A drastically less musical sound in this quarter is the piercing chant advertising the day's seafood specials—the caterwauling that helped give fishwives a bad name. Alfama can only be seen on foot: most streets are too narrow for anything but a donkey cart.

At the other end of the scale, the capital's central boulevard is wide enough for 12 traffic lanes and a couple of parkways. The Avenida da Liberdade, more than a century old, is often likened to the Champs-Ely-

Delicately carved, warm-coloured stone distinguishes great portal of historic monastery at Batalha.

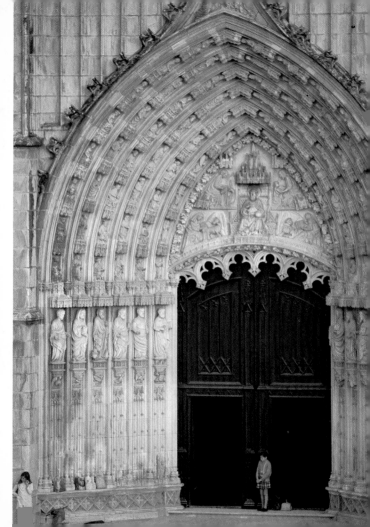

sées in Paris—except that the Lisbon version happens to have palm trees, duck ponds and mosaic pavements.

Elegant avenues and hilly alleys alike suffer from a very contemporary problem: the walls are often defaced by political graffiti and posters. As soon as they are erased, new slogans are scrawled, or occasionally painted artistically, with the demands of political parties and factions unaccustomed to the right of free speech. This is a recent innovation, dating back to the 1974 revolution which overthrew Portugal's long-standing dictatorship. Optimists consider

this temporary disfigurement a small price to pay for liberty.

The ubiquitous writing on the wall is strangely out of character for an unassuming people given to understatement. The Lisboans dress in conservative colours and styles. They never boast about their city or themselves. With such a

Portugal's changing times: plastic fishing lines in Sesimbra; political slogans that colour walls of Lisbon.

moderate temperament, they form bus queues even longer and more resigned than in London. They are kind, and often loving, towards animals. Portuguese bullfights spare the bull. **11**

You will get along with the Lisboans. They beam with delight if you try to speak two words of Portuguese. (If you manage a complete sentence they won't believe it.) Ask for directions and they make sure you don't go astray. Everyone will treat you with kindness and hospitality but no one—not a waiter, shoeshine boy or hotel maid—will stoop to subservience.

Sightseeing in Lisbon runs to monuments and parks, museums and churches—with a few surprises. The celebrated Tower of Belém, the landmark all the Portuguese explorers sought out as they came home, turns out to be half the size you expected. The stately church of São Vicente de Fora has a double-decker cloister lined with *azulejos*, painted tiles, which depict startlingly unmeditative scenes of hunting, sailing and the fables of La Fontaine.

Though you would expect to see museums of Portuguese history and art, you will also discover an array of international masterpieces assembled in a perfect Lisbon setting by the Armenian oil billionaire, Calouste Gulbenkian.

You'll want to get out of town, too, to take advantage of the green countryside and the beaches. A half-hour train ride takes you to the resorts of Estoril and Cascais, on the Costa do Estoril west of Lisbon. After a day of swimming, water-skiing and suntanning you can look into the nightclub and roulette situation at the Estoril Casino.

For more pastoral pleasures, see Sintra, one of Europe's prettiest towns. Even closer to Lisbon, the Versailles-style palace at Queluz is a "must"—unless a visiting head of state happens to be there. Or go on the cheapest excursion of all—a ferryboat to the south bank of the Tagus. You'll enjoy the excitement of the busy harbour and the enchanting views of Lisbon. And across the river stretches yet another fascinating region of vineyards, windmills and beaches, all within easy day-trips.

In your travels you'll discover good local specialities in the realm of food and drink: soups hearty enough for a sailor's homecoming, fish and seafood with just-caught flavour, and equally fresh fruits and vegetables. Every town seems to have its own copyrighted dessert, one sweeter than the next. As for wines, they're as unpretentious as the people you'll meet—and just as honest and memorable.

A Brief History

Of all the legends surrounding Lisbon's birth the most intriguing identifies the founding father as Ulysses. But hard-hearted historians don't take this paternity claim seriously. They are more inclined to place the city's origins around 800 B.C. with the establishment of a Phoenician trading station. Its name might have been Alis Ubbo or Olissipo, which contain the basic sounds of "Lisboa".

Nonetheless, primitive peoples, thousands of years earlier, had already settled in the area, so temptingly located on a calm river close to the sea. During the first thousand years B.C., Celtic tribes moved into northern and central Portugal.

Recorded history begins in the 3rd century B.C. when the Romans ousted the Carthaginians and created the province of Lusitania; Lisbon was proclaimed a full-fledged municipality. Julius Caesar is said to have named the town Felicitas Julia—more or less "Julius's Joy"—quite a compliment!

As Rome declined, the Iberian peninsula was overrun by Vandals and other unwelcome immigrants. The barbarians took Lisbon at the beginning of the 5th century. A series of migratory tribes controlled the city until the 6th-century arrival of the Visigoths, who provided peace.

The Moorish Conquest

In the year 711 a formidable invasion fleet from North Africa crossed the Strait of Gibraltar and conquered Iberia in the name of the Moslem religion. Lisbon soon fell beneath the Moorish steamroller. It became a thriving outpost of the peninsula's new management. Lisbon's oldest and most charming residential area, Alfama, retains the Arabic prefix "al" along with unpredictably twisting narrow streets as convoluted as a casbah.

Towards the end of the 8th century the Christian counter-attack began but with few lasting gains anywhere on Portuguese territory. Only in 1139, at the Battle of Ourique, did the tide turn. The victor of Ourique, Count Afonso Henriques of Portugal, became the country's first king. But Lisbon eluded his grasp for another eight years; the Moors were too securely ensconced in what is now the Castle of St. George.

In 1147 the king recruited a volunteer force of thousands of Norman, Flemish, German and English crusaders who were passing through on their way to the Holy Land. He convinced them to stay long enough to strike a blow against the Moslems and, perhaps no less gratifying, collect the booty of Lisbon.

The combined forces, Portuguese and crusaders, besieged Lisbon for four gruesome months. As the Moorish survivors fled, the victors surged in to grab the loot that was left behind. A century later the reconquest of Portugal was completed, and King Afonso III (1248–79) moved the national capital to Lisbon.

The Avis Dynasty

A decisive 14th-century battle was fought at Aljubarrota, about 100 kilometres north of Lisbon. João of Avis, recently proclaimed King João I of Portugal, assured independence from Spain by defeating the army of Juan I of Castile. Then Portugal cemented its alliance with Britain by the 1386 Treaty of Windsor, calling for eternal and true friendship. João of Avis took the pact so seriously that he married the daughter of

Monument on riverfront honours
14 *Henry the Navigator (far right).*

John of Gaunt, Philippa of Lancaster. Their third surviving son, the Duke of Viseu, Master of the Order of Christ, changed the map of the world. We know him better as Henry the Navigator.

Prince Henry won his spurs at 21 when he sailed from Lisbon with a daring expedition which captured the Moorish stronghold of Ceuta in 1415. It was his first and last act of derring-do. He retired to the "end-of-the-world", Sagres peninsula, and established a school of navigation in which he assembled astronomers, cartographers and other scientists who multiplied the skills of mariners. With single-minded determination, he organized expeditions that pushed back the horizon. During his lifetime Portuguese caravels sailed beyond the westernmost point of Africa. With the colonization of Madeira and the Azores the foundations of the future Portuguese empire were laid.

The king who ruled over Portugal's golden age of exploration—and exploitation—was Manuel I (1495–1521). The discoveries during his reign, compounding the profits already coming in from Madeira, the Azores and West Africa, made him Europe's richest ruler. He could well afford monuments as elegant as the Tower of Belém, as impressive as the Jerónimos Monastery. The style of architecture which eased Portugal from the Gothic into the Renaissance bears his name: whimsically flamboyant decorative touches, an exotic mixture of disparate elements—these are the trademarks of Manueline art.

The most significant expedition under Manuel's flag was Vasco da Gama's sea voyage from Lisbon in the summer of 1497. Rounding what is now called the Cape of Good Hope, he opened up East Africa and India to Portuguese traders. Da Gama actually found what Columbus had been looking for in the wrong direction—the sea-route to the spices of the East. In 1500 the Portuguese explorer Pedro Álvares Cabral opened another new epoch with his discovery of Brazil.

Times of Trial

Sixteenth-century Spain was gripped by witch-burnings, but Portugal accepted the Inquisition in its more moderate way. The first *auto-da-fe* in Lisbon did not occur until 1540, and the round-up of heretics never really attained major proportions. By the end of the century—in spite of the witch-hunt, earthquakes and an outbreak of plague—Lisbon had attracted so many country folk that the population was estimated at 100,000.

As a country with only two frontiers—the sea and the Spanish border—Portugal has an understandably keen interest in relations with its bigger neighbour. The worst happened in 1580 when Spain's King Philip II invaded the country and crowned himself Dom Filipe I of Portugal. At the National Museum of Coaches you can see the utilitarian cross-country carriage in which the monarch wearily but triumphantly travelled to Lisbon.

Returning from voyages, explorers yearned for sight of Belém tower.

It took 60 years for local forces to organize a successful uprising against the despised occupation. On December 1, 1640—the date is still celebrated as Portugal's Restoration Day—Spanish rule was finally overthrown. The Duke of Bragança was crowned King João IV in a joyful ceremony in Lisbon's enormous riverfront square, the Terreiro do Paço.

Morale was high in Portugal during the long reign of his grandson, João V (1706–50). As money poured in from the gold discoveries in Brazil, the king spent it on lavish monuments and public works projects. He built the remarkable aqueduct which still brings fresh water into the centre of Lisbon. His best-known extravagance was the palace and monastery at Mafra, 40 kilometres northwest of the capital. In another effort to enhance the grandeur of his court and country, the devout king convinced the pope to promote the see of Lisbon to a patriarchate. Religious passion permeated João's private life as well: his most notorious habit was a penchant for nuns.

Lisbon's Decimation

The great dividing line between early history and modern times in Portugal falls in the middle **18** of the 18th century. On All

Saints' Day, November 1, 1755, an earthquake devastated Lisbon. Churches, filled with worshippers, crumbled; overturned candles and lanterns spread fires throughout the city; and then a nightmarish tidal wave crashed ashore. The three-headed disaster killed between 15,000 and 60,000 people (sources differ drastically). Reminders of the nightmare are found in many parts of Lisbon to this day. The most dramatic is the wreckage of the

New generation studies Portugal's seafaring tradition in naval museum.

Carmelite church on a hill above the city's main square, open to the sky just as it was the morning the roof fell in.

Since routine problems of state were beyond the talents of the ineffective King José I (1750–77), he could hardly be expected to cope with the challenge of post-quake recovery. But the power behind the throne happened to be a tough, ambitious minister called Sebastião José de Carvalho e Mello, later elevated to be Count of Oeiras and (the name best remembered) the Marquis of Pombal. Taking advantage of the power vacuum, once the earth stopped shaking, Pombal mobilized all Portugal's resources for the clean-up. The survivors were fed and housed, the corpses disposed of, the ruins cleared. And then an ambitious project for a new city was laid out. Today the modern sections of the capital are referred to as Pombaline Lisbon.

Pombal's achievement is commemorated with his heroic statue atop a column at the north end of the Avenida da Liberdade. The choked traffic intersection is usually referred to as "Pombal". King José's huge equestrian statue holds the place of honour in the Praça do Comércio, where it was fawningly erected in his lifetime. The king had a close brush with death in an assassination attempt in 1758. Pombal reacted by inaugurating an unprecedented reign of terror, with public executions and widespread repression. José finally died of natural causes in 1777. The very next day the Marquis of Pombal was out of a job.

The Peninsular War

At the beginning of the 19th century, Napoleon dragged Portugal into the heat of Europe's conflicts. The situation became so perilous at one point that the royal family fled to Rio de Janeiro—and stayed there ten years after the crisis was over.

France was pressing Portugal to abandon its traditional loyalty to England. Lisbon tried to stay neutral in the struggle of the great powers. But in 1807 Napoleon demanded that Portugal do the impossible—declare war on Britain. Responding to the predictable veto, the French army marched on Portugal. For the next three years the country had to suffer military rule and all the indignities that go with it.

General Andoche Junot, who led the invasion, became the ruler of occupied Portugal. He had the good taste to set up headquarters in the gardened pink palace at Queluz. For months the people of Lisbon were demoralized at the sight of Napoleon's colours flying above the Castle of St. George.

But military miscalculations sent Junot's army packing later in 1808. Repeat engagements over the next two years turned into notable victories for the combined Portuguese-British force. They owed much to the strategic brilliance of an old Portugal hand—Sir Arthur Wellesley, the British commander, who became the Duke of Wellington. After the textbook battle of Torres Vedras, north of Lisbon, the French began a long, disastrous retreat.

Napoleon's last outpost in Portugal was evacuated in the spring of 1811.

Civil War

Only 22 years later the country was again at war—this time engaged in its most tragic variety, brother against brother. Pedro IV, formerly emperor of Brazil, fought to wrest the crown from his absolutist brother, Miguel I. Pedro won, but only a few months after his triumph he died of consumption. He was only 36 years old. His adolescent daughter, Maria da Glória, assumed the throne. She married a German nobleman, Ferdinand of Saxe-Coburg-Gotha, who built her the astonishing, romantic Pena Palace above Sintra and fathered her five sons and six daughters. Maria II died in childbirth at 34.

Premature and tragic deaths claimed many royal Portuguese, but in all the country's history only one king was assassinated. The victim was Carlos I, the date February 1, 1908. Like many other crucial events, it occurred in Lisbon's vast Terreiro do Paço (Praça do Comércio). As the royal family was riding past in an open carriage an assassin's bullet caught Carlos in the head. A few seconds later another conspirator fatally shot Carlos's son and heir, Prince Luíz Felipe. A third bullet hit the young prince Manuel in the arm. Thus wounded and haunted, Manuel II began a brief reign as Portugal's last king. He was deposed in October 1910 in a republican uprising by elements of the armed forces. The royal yacht took him to Gibraltar and later England, where he spent the rest of his life exiled in Twickenham.

Into Modern Europe

The republican form of government turned out to be as unstable as it was unfamiliar. Resignations, coups and assassinations kept a merry-go-round of presidents and prime ministers whirling. In the political and economic crisis, the nation could scarcely afford the luxury of war. But German threats to its African territories, among other motives, edged Portugal into World War I on the Allied side. On February 24, 1916, the Portuguese navy seized a group of German ships anchored in the Tagus and the Kaiser replied with the expected declaration of war. A Portuguese expeditionary force sailed for the trenches of France.

The war's toll hastened the end of the unsuccessful attempt at democracy. After a revolution in 1926, General António Óscar Carmona took over as strongman. Two years later he made his most fateful appointment, entrusting the economy to the hands of a professor named António de Oliveira Salazar. The exhausted Portuguese finances immediately perked up.

Political graffiti and murals blossomed after "red carnation" revolution.

In 1932 Dr. Salazar took over as prime minister. His tough authoritarian regime emphasized economic progress. He kept Portugal neutral in World War II, though permitting the Allies to use the Azores. Unlike his fellow-dictator across the border, Spain's Francisco Franco, Dr. Salazar avoided a personality cult; his portrait never graced the stamps or coins of his realm.

When a massive stroke felled Salazar in 1968, the reins were handed to a former rector of the University of Lisbon, Dr. Marcelo Caetano. Then in 1974 the armed forces overthrew the dictatorship in the dramatic "red carnation" revolution. Portugal disengaged from its seething African possessions and turned to healing its wounds and learning again how to live in a democracy.

Saints of Lisbon

Lisbon's favourite saint is known elsewhere as St. Anthony of Padua. Here, in his birthplace, the name is St. Anthony of Lisbon. He was born a few doors down the street from the cathedral, at the end of the 12th century. Preacher, theologian, patron of the poor, defender of human rights, he died in Italy in 1231.

The official patron saint of Lisbon is St. Vincent, a 4th-century martyr. The first king of Portugal, Afonso Henriques, ordered his remains shipped from the Algarve to Lisbon. Two ravens faithfully escorted the saintly relics, which explains why many a Lisbon lamp post is adorned with the wrought-iron symbol of a sailing ship with a bird fore and aft.

23

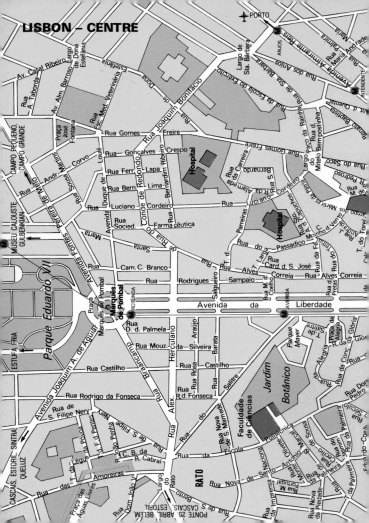

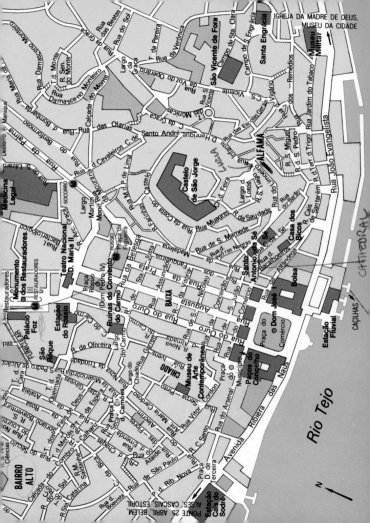

What to See

Lisbon's waterfront is an arc stretching nearly 20 miles. Most of the outstanding sights are within walking distance of the river, though (because of the hills or the lateral distances) not necessarily handy to each other.

You can travel efficiently and cheaply from place to place by public transport—the view from the top of a double-decker bus is hard to beat. For shorter trips, trams are useful; funiculars mount difficult hills. Lisbon's Metro—the underground railway or subway—is modern and fast but serves only

a limited area. Taxis are usually plentiful and always inexpensive. Traffic jams in Lisbon are not as fierce as in some of the bigger capitals but rush hour—about 8 to 10 a.m. and 5 to 7 p.m.—is best avoided.

When you arrive, sign up for a guided excursion or two, the fastest way to grasp the layout of any new city. Then you'll be ready to set forth on your own.

Our agenda of sights to savour begins with an elegant 18th-century square.

In city of hills, Edward VII park goes downhill towards the river; in Alfama, stair-climbers take a rest.

The Centre

The **Praça do Comércio** (Commerce Square) is one of the few really extravagant touches in a city of modest people and places. Stately pink arcades line three sides of the vast plaza; the fourth is open to the harbour, with Venetian-style stairs leading right into the Tagus.

Before the 1755 earthquake wiped out all the buildings around the plaza, it was called Terreiro do Paço (Palace Square)—the name by which it's still informally known. The haphazard pre-quake layout was less harmonious, but nowadays the square is such a beehive of cars, buses and trams that the regal effect is diminished.

The **statue** of a man in a plumed helmet on horseback represents King José I, patron of the great city-planner the Marquis of Pombal who designed the square. Another sculptural flourish is a triumphal arch connecting the government buildings on the north side of the square.

Through the arch you can see, or travel, the length of Rua Augusta, the main street of this rigidly rectangular 18th-century part of town. Critics find all those identically sized buildings monotonous, though

original decorative touches relieve some of the severity. After the 1755 disaster, all buildings on these 15 streets were built earthquake-proof. The area is called the **Baixa,** or lowland, and is full of banks, shops, small restaurants and teashops.

The top end of Rua Augusta

In lively Rossio district, old-fashioned cinema still attracts the fans.

runs into Lisbon's main square, the **Rossio.** In days gone by it was the scene of witch-burning and bullfights. It's still the very centre of activity of Lisbon—the place to meet friends, drink coffee, window-shop, watch the crowds, and listen to the fountains and the incomprehensible calls of the newsboys. The Rossio is also the most popular place to queue for a taxi or bus.

The statue atop the heroic **29**

column in this square honours Pedro IV of Portugal (1826–34), who was the first emperor of Brazil. A persistent legend maintains that it's not Pedro at all but a discarded statue of is doomed contemporary, Emperor Maximilian of Mexico, that turned up cheap at a surplus sale. Official sources deny this story.

The Rossio suburban railway station looks at first glance like a vision of a Moorish palace. Actually, it's a romantic effort of the late 19th century and the style is formally called neo-Manueline.

Confusingly, the Rossio sits side by side with another major square, the Praça da Figueira. This one is built around an equestrian statue of King João I, founder of the Avis dynasty.

Back to the Rossio and past the Teatro Nacional, a fairly straightforward obelisk marks the Praça dos Restauradores, which commemorates the overthrow of Spanish rule in 1640. A splendid palace on the west side of the square *(Palácio Foz)* houses the government's tourist information office. Opposite is a 24-hour post office.

From here the **Avenida da Liberdade** makes its well proportioned way uphill for about a mile. Among its fountains, statues, flower-gardens and ponds are benches from which to look up at the palm trees and down at the pavement mosaics. The boulevard ends at the traffic circle called Praça Marquês de Pombal, from which an elevated statue of the dictator (inexplicably accompanied by a ferocious lion) looks out over his works. In an ingenious reflection of the boulevard, a formal park continues uphill beyond Pombal. The manicured lawns and shrubs seem to be a northward extension of the avenue. On either side are informal forests and gardens. So thrilled were the Portuguese by a royal visit at the turn of the century that they named the park after England's Edward VII.

Lisbon's most original botanical triumph occupies the northwest corner of this park. Called the **Estufa Fria** ("cold greenhouse"), it's a tropical rain-forest in the heart of a European capital. Plants and flowers from Africa, Asia and South America feel right at home here in the Lisbon air, thanks to a simple system of slatted roofs and walls to filter the extremes of weather. Amidst moody pools and waterfalls, bananas grow big enough to eat (but too high to grab). A recent addition, a huge standard greenhouse, accommodates more delicate plants and trees. And the whole enterprise is surrounded by an open-to-nature display of Lisbon's indigenous flora.

Roof reflected in lotus pond keeps the atmosphere properly tropical for flamingos in Estufa Fria.

Old Lisbon

Almost every hill in town has a *miradouro* (belvedere), but the best panorama of all belongs to Lisbon's ancient castle. From the **Castelo de São Jorge** (St. George's Castle) you look out over the entire city, the river and the hills beyond the south

bank. The natural strategic value of this promontory is obvious. Roman soldiers may have built the first defensive walls on this spot about two thousand years ago.

The Moslems, who ruled Portugal from the 8th century, dug in well but they were finally dislodged in 1147. The new proprietors expanded the fortifications, but earthquakes and

Pigeons hitch a ride on statue of King João I outlined against restored fortifications of St. George's castle; costumed dolls wait for buyers.

less violent wear-and-tear over the following centuries left little intact. A serious restoration programme has given new life to the old ruins. The citadel and palace, ramparts and towers again tell their long, sometimes sad story.

Aside from the sensational vistas and the chance to roam the battlements, the castle is worth a visit just for its park. Platoons of birds strut around as if they own the place. Not just transient pigeons and sparrows but resident peacocks, pheasants, pelicans, flamingos, swans, geese and ducks. White and black are Lisbon's colours, so you'll see albino birds

and shiny black ravens—all watched over with affection by the municipality.

Dozens of Lisbon churches have historic or artistic merit, but we've tried to cut endless trudging and traipsing by mentioning only churches of unusual significance. The first in this survey, for geographical reasons—its twin towers rise above a hillside due east of the castle—is **São Vicente de Fora** (St. Vincent Beyond the Walls). Begun in the 16th century, this building is enormous by local standards, yet it succeeds in combining mass and grace.

It's all very Italianate, from the statues of saints in their niches on the façade to the baroque altar. The architect was an Italian, Filippo Terzi, who is said to have been inspired by the Jesuit church in Rome. St. Vincent's interior— a single nave and vaulted ceiling—has clean, crisp lines.

On the right, as you face the altar, a heavy wooden door leads to the monastic cloister— and a surprise. The walls are lined with *azulejos*, blue-and-white glazed tiles, depicting scenes of 18th-century French life and leisure, along with the animal fables of La Fontaine. On a non-frivolous note, have a look at the pantheon just off the cloister. It contains the tombs of

members of the royal Bragança family.

Behind the church, in the Campo de Santa Clara. Tuesdays and Saturdays are **market** days. On the fringes of the workaday clothing and housewares' stalls, antique collectors may uncover a valuable old clock, or at least a rusty steam iron. You wouldn't believe the range of second-hand items people will buy—or dare to put on sale—until you look over this flea market.

Just down the hill is the grandiose marble church of **Santa Engrácia,** with a high dome reminiscent of the Capitol building in Washington. Construction started in the 17th century, but what with one thing and another it wasn't finished until 1966. So, in Lisbon, describing something as the "works of Santa Engrácia" qualifies it as an endless job.

In the sumptuous rotunda, symbolic tombs salute the greatest men in Portuguese history; off to the side are real tombs of presidents of the republic. You can take an elevator up to the base of the dome for a dizzying view 250 feet straight down onto the marble floor of the rotunda. Outside is a terrace looking onto rooftops and the river.

Some old cities are built

around their cathedrals, set on a hill facing a square of sober civic buildings. Not Lisbon. Without so much as a proper plaza to set it off, the **cathedral** (*Sé*) of Lisbon just suddenly appears at a bend in the road. But don't misinterpret its invisibility; this is an impressive medieval cathedral with great historic and artistic importance.

It was begun as a fortress-church in the 12th-century; its towers, and walls with firing slits, still suggest a beleaguered citadel. Earthquakes badly damaged the church in the 14th, 16th and 18th centuries, so architectural touches range from Romanesque and Gothic to a bit of the baroque. One relic of the 18th century, the organ, still has a robust voice.

In one of the chapels you can see a couple of sentimental 14th-century **tombs.** The statue of a bearded old man, Lopo Fernandes Pacheco, lies on his sarcophagus with his hand on his sword, a favourite dog smiling at his feet; lying atop an adjacent stone coffin, a statue of his second wife reads her prayer book, accompanied by three devoted dogs.

For more medieval memories, ask to be admitted to the 13th-century **cloister.** There, amidst signs of earthquake damage, you can see parts of pre-Roman and Roman columns, statues and inscriptions. One old chapel has a brilliantly wrought iron screen with Moorish and Romanesque designs.

Just a few steps down the hill from the cathedral's main portal, the church of Santo António da Sé honours Lisbon's most revered native son. St. Anthony of Padua—known locally as St. Anthony of Lisbon—was born here in 1195. The crypt of this church was built on the spot where, according to local lore, his house stood. Among other roles, St. Anthony is the patron saint of girls looking for husbands; sometimes bridal bouquets are left at the altar of St. Anthony in the cathedral—with thanks for the good work.

Between here and the waterfront one last old building rates a glance. The **Casa dos Bicos** (House of Facets), built in the early 16th century, belonged to the family of the Duke of Albuquerque, viceroy of Portuguese India. The building is faced with stones shaped like pyramids. Before the 1755 earthquake the house of the protruding diamonds had four floors. Now it's down to two.

This street, Rua dos Bacalhoeiros (Street of the Cod-Sellers), is lined with fascinating **35** little shops. One sells nothing but corks for bottles and flasks of all sizes. Another is piled high with empty burlap sacks. Another's stock consists entirely of little cans of Portuguese sardines and tuna—thousands of them—with or without openers.

Which leads back to the waterfront square, Praça do Comércio. Any city with seagulls screeching at its gateway is bound to be colourful.

Alfama

All visitors agree: this is the most fascinating part of Lisbon, a labyrinth of crooked streets, stairways and alleys that go nowhere most deviously. Alfama is a chaos of tilting houses with mismatched windows, fish stalls and bars, laundry dripping onto the street, and the feeling that nothing has changed since the Middle Ages.

You will get lost. Even if you kept your nose in a map and consulted a compass (thereby missing all the sights), you would still get lost. Alfama is a cartographer's nightmare, with roads going over and under each other and ending in blank walls. You would need a scale model to make sense of it, and a mountain goat's talents to get around.

The only solution is to tour by trial and error. When in doubt, stick to the narrow streets. If you find yourself in a conventional street wide enough for both a car and a pedestrian, you've strayed from Alfama.

You could start wandering at the southern extremities of the neighbourhood—Largo do Chafariz de Dentro or Largo do Terreiro do Trigo. It's easier, though, to start from the top, at Largo do Salvador or Largo das Portas do Sol, and let gravity lead you back down towards the river.

Here are a few of Alfama's highlights. You might be lucky enough to discover some of them through an arch or round a blind corner. If not, come back another day for more of the intriguing sights, sounds and smells of Alfama.

Rua de São João da Praça: this is where Portugal's first king, Afonso I, entered Lisbon through the Moorish wall on October 25, 1147.

Igreja de São Miguel (St. Michael's Church): built in the 12th century, restored in the 18th, with a glorious ceiling

Cobblestone paths lead through the medieval labyrinth of Alfama.

of Brazilian jacaranda wood. It's dark inside, but the caretaker will turn on the lights so that you can see the rococo gilt altar screen.

Beco da Cardosa: an alley with blind-alley offshoots, the very essence of the higgledy-piggledy delights of Alfama.

Igreja de Santo Estêvão (St. Stephen's Church): 13th-century octagonal floor-plan, but rebuilt several times over the years. The overhanging back of the church nearly collides with

the front gate of an old palace.

Beco do Carneiro (Sheep Alley): ancient houses sag towards each other across a step-street wide enough for one-and-a-half pedestrians. Look up: it's not a trick of perspective, the eaves of the buildings really do touch.

Rua de São Pedro: Alfama's boisterous main shopping street, too narrow for cars. Fruits and vegetables are cheaper than downtown; fish-wives shriek; chickens, dogs

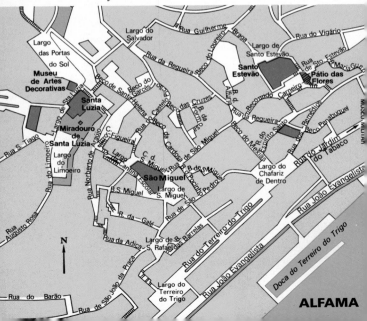

ALFAMA

and children get in everyone's way.

Largo de São Rafael: remains of a tower, part of the Moorish defences which were finally overwhelmed in 1147.

Bairro Alto

Like Alfama, the Bairro Alto ("high neighbourhood") is a hilly section full of evocative old houses with wrought-iron balconies occupied by birdcages and flowerpots. At night the district's restaurants, loaded with atmosphere, and *fado* nightclubs attract visitors from afar. There are disco bars with a clientele of sailors and other itinerants in search of X-rated diversion.

Whatever your pleasure—though here we deal with historic monuments—the easiest way to reach the Bairro Alto is to board the eccentric yellow **funicular** trolley at Praça dos Restauradores. The ticket may be the cheapest thing you can buy in all Portugal, but the hill is walkable if you're on an emergency budget or need the exercise.

At the top end of the brief journey the city council has built a lookout park called the Miradouro de São Pedro de Alcântara. Though you can see no more than a slice of the river, the **panorama** includes a good view of the castle of St. George head-on across the valley. A tile orientation table, slightly out of date, helps you identify the landmarks.

Two churches in this part of town are unusual enough to rate your attention. Just down the street from the park is the **Igreja de São Roque** (Church of St. Rock). Don't be put off by its uninteresting exterior—the original 16th-century façade perished in the great 18th-century quake—because inside you will see the most lavishly decorated chapels in Lisbon. A couple of them are so baroque you'll hardly believe that angels could stay afloat amidst golden swirls in such profusion. The **altar** of the chapel of São João Baptista (St. John the Baptist), on the left, is a wealth of gold, silver, bronze, amethyst, agate, lapis lazuli, ivory and Carrara marble. In 1742 King João V of Portugal sent off a mail-order to Rome, where teams of artists and artisans worked on this altar for five years. Then the pope gave his blessing and the altar was dismantled and shipped to the customer, an incredible prefabricated masterpiece.

Alongside the church, the Museu de Arte Sacra (Museum of Sacred Art) contains a collec-

tion of precious reliquaries, delicately worked jewellery and vestments.

Downhill from here, the **Igreja do Carmo** (Carmelite Church) is rich only in memories. It was built in the 14th century. As you stand on the grass inside the shell of what was one of Lisbon's great churches of the age, look up through the arches into the blue sky and imagine the scene that day in 1755 when the pillars rocked and the roof fell in on a full congregation.

Inside the part of the church which is still roofed they've organized a modest archaeological museum—a hodgepodge of prehistoric pottery, Roman sculpture, early Portuguese tombs and even—brace yourself—a few ancient mummies under glass.

The fastest way to reach the centre of town from here is the **Elevador de Santa Justa,** a vertical variation of the funiculars used elsewhere in town. This lift, inaugurated in 1901, was originally powered by steam. It's 100 feet high and quite a remarkable sight in itself.

Just off the Rossio, tired shoppers can save steps by riding the lift, a wonder of Victorian technology.

The longer, slower, more picturesque way downhill is to wander the streets of the district called the **Chiado.** Lisbon's best shopping streets descend in a zigzag path from the Praça Luís de Camões to the Rossio. Among shops selling silverware, leather, fashions and books nestle elegant pastry and tea shops. And of course if you walk you save the price of the lift ticket, a down-payment on tea and cakes.

A Poet's Saga

Like his Spanish contemporary, Cervantes, Portugal's greatest literary figure knew prison, war and suffering first-hand.

Luís Vaz de Camões (1524–80)—Camoens in English—lost his right eye in a battle for the North African outpost of Ceuta. Shipwrecked off Indochina in 1558, he swam to safety with one arm; the other held aloft the manuscript of his most imperishable work, the *Lusiadas.* This book-length poem, patterned on a Homeric epic, tells the saga of the Portuguese explorers.

After Camões died, in near poverty, his fame multiplied. So did his poetry. Posthumous sonnets—apocryphal or outright forgeries—more than tripled the number of his published works.

Belém

As the seagull flies, Belém (Portuguese for Bethlehem) lies about 6 kilometres west of Pombal's Praça do Comércio. This Lisbon district has more than its share of monuments and museums. Land has been reclaimed from the river to provide parkland and marinas, so the shore itself is unrecognizable; but this is the place from which the great Portuguese discoveries of the 15th and 16th centuries were launched.

To save the most beautiful for last, we suggest starting a visit to Belém at the edge closest to central Lisbon. The **Museu Nacional dos Coches** (National Coach Museum) is housed, aptly, in the former riding school of the Belém Royal Palace. Two great halls display dozens of horsedrawn carriages for city or ceremonial or rugged cross-country travel over four centuries of European history. The exhibition starts with a 16th-century monster in which King Philip II of Spain was transported in triumph—and doubtless in discomfort—to Spanish-ruled Portugal in 1580. The most extravagant are three sculpted, gilt carriages used by the Portuguese embassy in Rome in the early 18th century to impress Pope Clement XI.

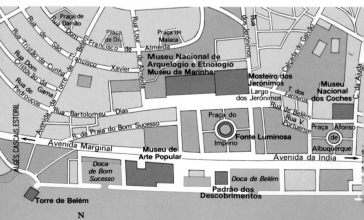

One coach after another illustrates the painfully slow evolution of technical details leading up to the sleek 19th-century Crown Carriage, still worthy of any royal procession. In this museum, called the world's greatest collection of coaches, nothing's been overlooked—not even the regal riding accessories from stirrups to coach-horns.

A short stroll westward along the Rua de Belém leads to Lisbon's biggest and most admirable religious monument, the **Mosteiro dos Jerónimos.** This monastery was begun by Manuel I with the riches Portuguese ships brought back from the East. The convent wing was shattered in the 1755 earthquake but the world is lucky that the church and cloister he ordered built still survive. They are moving testaments to 16th-century faith and taste.

Stop and look at the vast south façade of the church, parallel to the riverbank. Much of the vertical area is unadorned limestone, but when embellishments occur they really sing out. The main portal is a wonder of intricate stonework. Inside the church, columns carved in designs of the Manueline era (which bridged the gap between Gothic and Renaissance styles

in Portugal) contribute to a feeling of infinite height and space. The first architect in charge was a Frenchman named Boytac; he was succeeded by the Spaniard João de Castilho.

Though it's usually quite dark inside the church you'll probably be able to pick out several royal tombs, set atop pompous sculptured elephants in a bizarre tribute to the newly discovered marvels of the East.

Near the west door are the modern tombs of two other giants of Portugal's golden age, Vasco da Gama and the poet Luís de Camões.

Once out of the church (don't miss the fine sculptural work surrounding the exterior of the west portal) turn right for the cloister. This is an airy double-decker structure with most original proportions. As you stroll round the arcades the very dimensions of the place seem to change because of the clever intersection of angles and arches. No two columns are alike.

It may be an anticlimax, but the western part of the monastery has been restored and now contains the **Museu Nacional de Arqueologia e Etnologia** (National Museum of Archaeology and Ethnology). This is the definitive collection **43** of Portuguese relics—primitive tools and jewels and, from the Roman days, excellent sculptures and mosaics.

The educational attractions continue just to the west with a planetarium, contributed by Portugal's ubiquitous benefactor, Calouste Gulbenkian.

Next door, the **Museu da Marinha** (Naval Museum) ought to interest anyone who cares about history or the sea. Children are fascinated by models of sailing ships, often fiendishly intricate. (Signs in the museum order that all children be led by the hand "to avoid disasters and damage".) The most startling exhibit is a galliot or brigantine built in 1785 to celebrate a royal marriage, with 80 oarsmen in red jackets—dummies—poised to row.

The ship models, scores of them, trace sea travel from the earliest caravels to modern liners and warships. Plenty of ancient anchors, charts, cannon and uniforms—even lighthouse lamps—provide footnotes.

Between the monastery and the river is a large garden with rose beds, bird of paradise flowers and swan ponds. The Fonte Luminosa (luminous fountain) can be hooked up to provide a 45-minute show of changing light and colour patterns.

The modern **Padrão dos Descobrimentos** (Monument to the Discoveries) juts from the riverbank like a caravel cresting a wave. On the prow stands Prince Henry the Navigator, wearing, as always, his funny round hat. The statues behind him, on both sides of the central shaft, represent noted explorers, mapmakers, astronomers, chroniclers and others he mobilized in the dauntless days of discovery.

A compass and map of the world inlaid in the pavement here shows the phenomenal extent of Portugal's exploration in the golden age, from the Azores and Brazil to India and Macao.

One more museum to mention in this immediate waterfront area: the **Museu de Arte Popular** (Popular Art Museum) surveys the folk art and customs of Portugal, according to regions. Plenty of charming fabrics, furniture, embroidery, toys and dolls.

And finally to the **Torre de Belém.** Sighting it on their return from a year or two at sea, the weary explorers felt deep

Tourists of all ages appreciate Manueline details in cloister of Lisbon's monastery of Jerónimos.

44

emotion. So may you. It's wonderfully graceful and imaginative. The details are probably familiar from pictures, but the tower is much smaller than you may have imagined: it's just a jewel.

Wander around the waterfront park and consider the poetry that sunlight outlines on the finely carved details of the fort. You can cross the moat and enter a 16th-century world, though the interior is unexpectedly austere. The most handsome aspect is the side facing the river, with a lovely loggia.

A 19th-century Portuguese writer, Ramalho Ortigão, conceded that the tower had no importance as a military construction, but he suggested a secret weapon: "The only defensive arm the tower of Belém can use against an enemy is its beauty."

Rising sun silhouettes monument to Portuguese explorers, bridge across the Tagus and fishermen.

Landmarks and Lookouts

Here we consider monuments you can see from many parts of Lisbon. And some places to go for the best view of them.

The **Ponte 25 de Abril** fills three roles: it's a major landmark, a lookout point and the way to get to another top landmark and lookout point. Europe's longest suspension bridge, it was opened to traffic in 1966 and named in honour of the nation's dictator. After the revolution of 1974 the word "Salazar" was removed and for quite a time it was awkwardly called just "the bridge". Finally it was named after the date of that revolution, April 25.

The bridge over the Tagus may not be the most graceful to look at, but the view *from* the bridge is extremely impressive. Facing Lisbon it's nearly as dramatic as the vista from an airliner.

Just across the river, looming

over the bridge's toll booths, is Lisbon's variation on Rio de Janeiro's trademark, the statue of **Christ the King.** More than 90 feet tall, it stands atop a modern four-pronged pedestal. A church, the Santuário de Cristo-Rei, is housed in the base of the monument. Take the lift to the viewing terrace for a perfectly glorious 360-degree **panorama** of the whole Tagus estuary, the bridge, all Lisbon and a vast expanse of Portugal to the south.

To visit the statue you can drive across the bridge or take one of the **ferryboats** from Praça do Comércio to Cacilhas and then a taxi or a bus marked "Cristo-Rei". The ferryboat, in any case, is strongly recommended for its exciting introduction to the port. The commuters may read their newspapers oblivious to the view, but you'll enjoy the ferry's manœuverings among ocean liners, freighters, tankers, warships and tugs. It's the definitive fisherman's-eye view of Lisbon. Merchant ships sail from here to the old Portuguese territories—from Rio de Janeiro to Maputo—and wherever else the sea lanes lead.

You may get on the wrong ferryboat on the way back from Cacilhas. No problem. Its destination is Lisbon's Cais do Sodré, only a few hundred yards west of Praça do Comércio, and something worth seeing. The railway station here is the place to catch a commuter train for Estoril and Cascais. In this nautical neighbourhood the stores sell full-size anchors, compasses, buoys and engine-room telegraphs—really serious maritime equipment, obviously not for the Sunday sailor. This is also the site of Portugal's biggest **market,** known as the Mercado da Ribeira, where more than a thousand people work. Men in padded caps balance unwieldy wicker trays of fruits and vegetables on their heads. Since it's both a wholesale and retail market something colourful is always going on from 2 a.m. to 9 p.m. But the best time to absorb the atmosphere is before lunch. You might just pick up the makings for a great picnic, too.

Lisbon's biggest landmark keeps popping into your field of vision from the most unexpected places, in and outside of town. Not surprising when you consider it's 11 miles long. The **aqueduct** of Águas Livres may remind you of ancient Rome, but it's a more recent engineering feat: the water began pouring into the fountains of central Lisbon in 1748. It still does.

*City's waterfront evokes memories
of the former Portuguese empire.*

The motorway and the aqueduct go through the city's biggest park, **Monsanto.** Eucalyptus, cypress, cedar and oak trees thrive on the rolling hillsides.

Aside from calm, beauty and fresh air the park is well supplied with amenities—sports grounds, bars and restaurants. Its municipal camping ground ranks as one of Europe' prettiest and best organized. Finally, the park has some outstanding *miradouros* (lookout points) over Lisbon and the estuary.

49

One last belvedere deserves special mention: the **Miradouro de Santa Luzia** on the edge of Alfama. From the tiled balcony perched on a bluff you look straight down onto a charming jumble of tiled roofs. In the little park here, old men in black berets take the sun, play cards and look at the tourists with good-natured curiosity. Look for two remarkable *azulejos*, tile panels, on the wall facing the belvedere. One shows Lisbon's waterfront as it looked before the great earthquake. The other depicts with bloodthirsty detail the rout of the Moors from the Castle of St. George in 1147.

Museums: Essential

Lisbon's most wondrous museum was created to house the thousands of works of art acquired by the Armenian billionaire Calouste Gulbenkian. A visit to the pleasant modern gallery will also tell you a lot about this great philanthropist, who died in Lisbon in 1955. Clearly he knew what he liked and was willing to pay any price to get it. He must have been the terror of all museum directors bidding against him.

The collection of the **Gulbenkian Museum** starts, chronologically, with Egyptian ceramics and sculptures going back to 2700 B.C. They are so rare and so perfectly preserved that they are simply awesome. The handsome statue of the Judge Bes is inscribed with hieroglyphs which date it from the reign of Pharaoh Psamtik I (7th century). Notice the life-like bronze statuettes of cats and kittens.

You don't have to know anything about numismatics to admire the collection of gold and silver coins from ancient Greece. A 6th-century B.C. coin was minted by that noted gold enthusiast Croesus. A set of medallions on show here may have been prizes at the Olympic Games of A.D. 242.

A large section of the museum is devoted to the art of the Islamic East—the rarest ancient fabrics, carpets and costumes, plus ceramics, glassware and illuminated pages from the

Blue-and-white azulejos decorate garden off Largo de Santa Luzia. **51**

Koran. The picture windows here show the art of landscaping; the museum is surrounded by its own perfectly planned and maintained park.

Gulbenkian's survey of Western art begins in the 11th century with illuminated parchment manuscripts. Exquisite ivory sculptures of religious scenes come from 14th-century France. There are well-preserved tapestries from Flemish and Italian workshops of the 16th century.

When you finally stumble across the Rembrandts, you'll feel it was inevitable that Gulbenkian would have acquired a pair. There's the portrait of a helmeted warrior believed to be Pallas Athena and *Figure of an Old Man.* Other masterpieces by Dutch and Flemish artists of the same era surround them.

The French collection shines in the area of furniture, tapestries and goldsmith's art from the 18th century, plus paintings by Watteau and Fragonard. British art includes works by Gainsborough and Turner.

One room is dedicated to the 18th-century Venetian artist, Francesco Guardi. The collection of his 19 *vedute* (views) and *capricci* (caprices) of Venice is considered the finest anywhere. The French Impressionists

are represented by Monet, Manet, Renoir and Degas. Two of the most charming are Manet's *Boy with Cherries* and *Boy Blowing Bubbles.*

Just when you think Gulbenkian is running out of surprises you discover that he was also something of an expert on Oriental art. The hall of Chinese porcelains starts with the Yuan epoch (the time of Marco Polo) and goes on to these exquisite 17th- and 18th-century items. As everywhere in the museum, each piece represents the pinnacle of a particular school of art, miraculously unmarred over centuries.

The last room of the museum must have been close to Gulbenkian's heart. It contains 169 items by his friend René Lalique (1860–1945), the versatile French artist who seems to sum up Art Nouveau. Here are pendants, bracelets, necklaces and combs of assorted materials and unexpected motifs— serpents, crickets, beautiful women. lovers, butterflies and owls. Each piece has a built-in surprise.

The museum is only one element of the Calouste Gul-

Gulbenkian museum starts with ancient artefacts; foundation also maintains orchestra and choir.

Museum Finder

Most Lisbon museums are open Tuesdays to Sundays from about 10 a.m. to 5 p.m.

Here are Lisbon's top ten museums with correct Portuguese titles and addresses. Be sure to check local listings for any seasonal modifications in opening hours.

Ancient Art—Museu Nacional de Arte Antiga, Rua das Janelas Verdes. Open later Thursdays and Sundays. Free on weekends.

Archaeology (Carmo)—Museu Arqueológico, Convento do Carmo, Largo do Carmo.

Coaches—Museu Nacional dos Coches, Praça Afonso de Albuquerque, Belém. Open later in summer.

Decorative Arts—Museu Escola de Artes Decorativas (Fundacão Ricardo Espirito Santo Silva), Largo das Portas do Sol 2, Alfama. Closes 1–2 p.m. weekdays; on Sundays, closed in the morning.

Folk Art—Museu de Arte Popular, Avenida Brasília, Belém.

Gulbenkian—Museu Calouste Gulbenkian, Avenida de Berna at Praça de Espanha. Hours change in summer. Free on weekends.

Military—Museu Militar, Largo dos Caminhos de Ferro. Opens later on Sundays.

Naval—Museu da Marinha, Praça do Império. Admission free on Wednesdays.

Religious Art—Museu de Arte Sacra, next to São Roque, Largo Trindade Coelho. Free on Sundays.

Tiles—Museu do Azulejo, Convento da Madre de Deus. Closes 1–2.30 p.m. Gratis.

benkian Foundation. Elsewhere on the premises are concert and exhibition halls, a library, a bookstore and a comfortable snack-bar.

The **Museu Nacional de Arte Antiga** (National Museum of Ancient Art) is in a big palace improbably set almost alongside the Lisbon docks. If you get lost, ask for "Janelas Verdes" (green shutters), the street it's on and also the name by which the palace and the museum are better known.

Three items in this museum are just about worth a trip to Lisbon in themselves:

1. *The Adoration of St. Vincent* from Lisbon's convent of São Vicente de Fora, attributed to the 15th-century Portuguese master, Nuno Gonçalves. Composed of six large panels, it contains recognizable portraits of contemporary dignitaries, including Henry the Navigator, looking properly devout. But

dozens of other faces are shown in every range of distraction—boredom, amusement, ire. A number of the assembled clergymen look ugly, evil or both. The lifelike faces in the crowd make this a classic of Portuguese art.

2. *The Temptation of St. Anthony* by Hieronymus Bosch. Painted around 1500, this fantastic piece of Bosch hallucination is tempered with humour and executed with genius. A crane rigged up like a helicopter, walking fish, animal-faced men and the most hideous disasters fill this unbelievably imaginative triptych.

3. A collection of 16th-century Japanese screens. You might miss these, in a small room all by themselves, but don't leave Lisbon until you've found them. The arrival of the Portuguese in Japan, as seen through Japanese eyes, is the theme of these extraordinary historical documents. Almost all the foreigners are portrayed rather villainously and the "natives", watching from their pagodas, appear to be amused. Who wouldn't be, at the sight of these strangely garbed, long-nosed grandees with their fawning servants, folding chairs and even, in one case, sunglasses?

All three of these Janelas Verdes triumphs are full of fascinating details, so you'll have to force yourself to move on to other parts of the museum. There's much more to see: English, Flemish, French, Dutch, German, Italian and Spanish paintings of the 14th to 19th centuries, most meticulously restored—perhaps too new-looking to be wholly satisfying; china and glassware from Europe and the Orient; rare Portuguese furniture and tapestries; and a bequest by Calouste Gulbenkian—a room of ancient sculpture, up to his admirable standards, including a Greek torso of marble from the 5th century B.C. and a statue of a lion from the palace of Emperor Tiberius at Capri. By now we would expect no less of the great collector.

More Museums—and a Palace

The **Convento da Madre de Deus** (Convent of the Mother of God) contains one of Lisbon's most memorable churches as well as an important museum. It's a bit out of the way, though, a mile or so northeast of anything else a tourist might want to look at (see map on p. 62). But it's worth the effort.

55

Founded at the beginning of the 16th century, the convent needed a top-to-bottom reconstruction after the great 18th-century earthquake. The interior of the re-done church is

Works in Madre de Deus illuminate the history of religion and art.

overpoweringly rich. Someone had the original idea of covering the side walls with blue and white painted tiles from Holland; two rows of enormous paintings hang above them, and the ceiling is full of paintings, too. Everywhere in the church the décor is a frenzied mixture of the most florid gilt

woodwork, paintings and precious old tiles.

The **Museu do Azulejo,** a museum devoted entirely to the art of painted tiles, occupies much of the adjoining convent building. This includes a miniature double-decker cloister surrounded by tiles in Moorish-style geometric patterns. By official count about 12,000 *azulejos* are exhibited here, ranging from 15th-century polychrome designs to 20th-century Art Deco. Don't miss the *Great Lisbon Panorama*, a picture 120 feet long composed of painted tiles, recording every detail of Lisbon's riverside as it looked 25 years before the earthquake. On a lighter note, seven whimsical panels show the rags-to-riches biography of an early-19th-century hatmaker.

In the **Museu de Artes Decorativas** (Decorative Arts Museum) an old palace has been filled with the choicest pieces of furniture, ceramics, silver and carpets from 16th- to 19th-century Portugal and the Portuguese empire. Fine examples of woodworking are arrayed in rooms that often look lived-in. Among the curiosities: a primitive version of a fold-up sofa-bed; children's rooms with mini-furniture; and an 18th-century picnic basket fit for a hungry king. The museum, and an attached school for cabinet-makers, bookbinders, engravers and other artisans, belongs to the Ricardo Espírito Santo Silva Foundation. Inconveniently, the palace—just above the Miradouro de Santa Luzia, the lookout point from which you survey the roofs of Alfama —is unmarked.

Lisbon's **Museu Militar** (Military Museum) is on the site of a foundry where 16th-century cannon were cast (see map on p. 25). The weapons now on show date much further back: crossbows, maces and lashes; 14th-century mortars; and even Vasco da Gama's two-handed sword, as tall as a man. The age of chivalry is represented by many suits of armor, custom-made for knights and their horses. A large, evidently nostalgic section specializes in World War I— snapshots of Portuguese troops at the front, faded medals, bugles and helmets with bullet-holes as souvenirs. The patio of this building overflows with cannon and even a tank. The museum is a handy place to while away an hour if you're waiting for a train at the Santa Apolónia station, across the square.

The **Palácio da Ajuda,** the biggest palace inside the city **57** limits, brims with art-works and curiosities. Portugal's King Luís I (1861–89) and his bride, Princess Maria Pia of Savoy, became the first royal family to live there; they deserve the credit for the fine furnishings —Gobelin tapestries, oriental ceramics and rare old Portuguese furniture. Behind a façade resembling a scaled-down Buckingham Palace there are three dining rooms: one for state occasions seats 50, the upstairs dining room is suitable for feeding 160 close friends, while the intimate but still lavish family snack spot comes with a billiard room attached. Guides point out down-to-earth novelties like the queen's sewing machine in a special rococo case and the queen's bathroom with made-in-England ("tip to empty") wash-basins.

More Parks and Gardens

Because it is set in a lovely park, Lisbon's **Jardim Zoológico** has been called Europe's most beautiful zoo. Another endearing element: a sense of humour. One of the big chimpanzee cages is designed as a wine store with kegs, unbreakable bottles and scales—the setting for spirited scampering.

The star of the show in this zoo is a money-spinning elephant who rings a bell and blows a horn when you hand him a coin. Children are well taken care of, with their own little amusement park and a driving school with foot-powered cars. Feeding time for the animals is 4 p.m.; children munch all day thanks to a choice of snack bars, a restaurant, and pushcart treats.

The **Jardim Botânico** (Botanical Garden), alongside the Academy of Sciences, goes in for the scientific cultivation of unusual plants from distant climes. But this serious activity doesn't disturb the lush beauty and overall tranquillity.

Campo Grande, between the zoo and the airport, is a popular park with Lisboans. Palm, cedar and willow trees shade pretty walks and a small lake with rowing boats.

A perfectly delightful park officially called Jardim Guerra Junqueiro is unofficially known as **Estrela** (star), the name of the distinguished 18th-century church across the street (see map on p. 62). Abundant tropical foliage plus the customary ducks, geese, peacocks and pheasants—and a belvedere offering yet another angle on the city and its harbour.

Excursions

Estoril Coast

The Costa do Estoril (formerly called Costa do Sol) begins just west of Lisbon in a commuter-and-resort town of less than global renown, CARCAVELOS. It goes all the way around the tip of the peninsula to Guincho on the open Atlantic. In the middle of all this, 25 kilometres from Lisbon, is the elegant and celebrated resort with the big reputation, Estoril.

For most foreign tourists the half-hour train ride from Cais do Sodré station in Lisbon to Estoril goes through irrelevant, anonymous towns. Alas, nothing we can do will glamorize PAÇO DE ARCOS or SANTO AMARO. But speeding past by train or car, have a look at the villas and their gardens in some of these obscure settlements. No matter what the map says, it's all very Mediterranean.

The railway station at **Estoril** is right alongside the beach. On the other side of the tracks (and across the coast road) is a formal park with carefully studied ranks of palms, disciplined shrubs, flower-beds and ponds. The park acts as the front lawn of the town's most imposing building, the new **casino.** With its nightclub, restaurants, bars, cinema, exhibition halls, shops and gambling rooms this is Estoril's one-stop after-dark amusement centre.

In spite of the modern décor the casino, which employs about 200 croupiers, maintains an old-fashioned pace. Gambling—roulette, baccarat, blackjack, craps and a Portuguese game called French Bank—is suspended only two nights a year: Good Friday and Christmas Eve. Legend says somebody broke the bank one Good Friday, prompting a superstitious management to declare it a holiday thenceforth. But officials dismiss the story as a figment of wishful thinking. If you have any money left, you can try one of the 300 or so slot-machines on your way out.

The town of Estoril is as discreet as a big winner ought to be. Victorian villas and some sleek modern mansions are tucked away behind green curtains of palms, eucalyptus, pines and vines. Since the turn of the century many a monarch, suddenly unemployed, has gravitated to Estoril or Cascais to dream about restoration in luxurious privacy.

As early as the mid-18th century Estoril was attracting visitors because of its balmy climate and the thermal baths, which were considered good for liver complaints. But prehistoric travellers got there a lot earlier. Among other things, they built a couple of cave-cemeteries in Estoril. These were discovered in 1944, not far from the beach, dug out of the limestone. Along with skulls and bones and artefacts, four gold rings in spiral form were found; you can see them at the museum in Cascais.

While Estoril is all resort—cosmopolitan and sybaritic—**Cascais** lives a dramatic double life. It has been called the town of fishermen and kings. Indeed, simple men of the sea coexist admirably with the lords of local villas and camera-slung tourists.

Something's always going on at the fishermen's beach, even on holidays when the little blue, yellow or red boats are ashore. A few fishermen in Sunday suits, uneasy in shoes and neckties, trade stories. The seagulls stand around taking the sun and local children turn the beach into a football field.

The workaday fishing scene attracts tourists who inspect the catch as it is unloaded from the boats into wooden trays, then rushed to the modern auction

building. There the fish is sold by a reverse auction, in which the price starts high and decreases until somebody shouts a bid. You may not understand the auctioneer's chant, but you'll like the looks of what he's selling—lobster, shrimp, hake, sardines and squid. The retail sales are in the hands of local fishwives set up outside the market. For the finished product, try any of the dozen or so restaurants within walking distance of the beach.

The **main square** of Cascais is a charmer. The Paços do Concelho (town hall) has stately windows with wrought-iron railings, separated by panels of *azulejos* picturing saints. The fire department occupies a place of honour between the town hall and a disused but attractive church. And in the main square, with undulating designs in its mosaic pavement, stands a modern statue of King Pedro I, crowned tall and majestic.

The forbidding 17th-century fort, called the Cidadela (citadel), is one of the few buildings to have survived the earthquake and tidal wave of 1755. In a small chapel within the walls is an image of St. Anthony, traditionally borne on the back of a white mule during parades.

Bundled against autumn breezes on Costa do Estoril, locals peer at bathers on Carcavelos beach.

ESTORIL COAST

After an overdose of sun and salt, the municipal park down the road is a cool relief. Under towering trees white swans comb their feathers alongside ponds brimming with prosperous-looking red and silver fish. The palace in this park is a museum—the **Museu dos Condes de Castro Guimarães**—with archaeological remains, art works, old furniture and gold and silversmith items. One prize exhibit is a 16th-century illuminated manuscript with a detailed picture of Lisbon harbour in the time of the great discoveries.

The road west passes **Boca do Inferno** (Mouth of Hell), a geological curiosity in which the force of the ocean is dramatically displayed. When tides are rough the crashing waves send up astonishingly high spouts of spray, accompanied by ferocious sound-effects.

The Costa do Estoril officially ends at the tip of the peninsula at **Guincho**, where there's a choice of breakers-against-rocks or a restful sand beach. Just up the coast you can see a formidable cape, **Cabo da Roca**, the westernmost point of all Europe.

Vacationers on the Costa do Estoril enjoy all the usual sports on land and sea as well as a sophisticated nightlife. In addition there are events for specialized tastes: show-jumping, car-racing, an experimental theatre, a jazz festival and bullfights. The mean temperature on this coast is 70° F. in summer, 52° in winter: mild enough any time of year for a holiday—or, if it comes to that, stylish exile.

Queluz

Here's an easy half-day outing to a pretty pink palace in the country, 14 kilometres west of Lisbon. Coach tours include Queluz, or you can drive yourself, leaving Lisbon on the motorway through the forest of Monsanto. After a brief look at the gentle hills and pastureland west of Lisbon, you're alongside the sprawling palace. Or you can take a commuter train, from Rossio station to Queluz.

The **palace** was built in the second half of the 18th century under the direction of two talented architects: the Portuguese Mateus Vicente de Oliveira and Frenchman Jean-Baptiste Robillon. As a working official residence for the royal family, Queluz thrived mostly during the reign (1777–99) of Maria I. However, the unfortunate queen, best remembered for her madness, failed to enjoy the place during her frequent fits of depression.

From the highway side, the palace seems relatively unprepossessing, but Portuguese modesty is abandoned on the inside. Logically, the **throne room** is the most lavish hall of all, with overpowering chandeliers and walls and ceilings burdened with gilt. The Hall of Ambassadors has a floor like a huge chessboard, many mirrors, and thrones at the far end. Actually, Queluz is curiously laid out with public rooms bordering living quarters almost incoherently.

The **gardens,** pride of Queluz, go on and on with clipped hedges in geometric array and bushes barbered into inventive shapes. Huge old magnolia trees relieve some of the formality; nearby are enough orange trees to keep any queen well supplied with marmalade. (But don't pick the fruit—it belongs to the government!) Royal guests would enter the garden via the pompous but original **Escadaria dos Leões** (Lions' Staircase). The fountains in the garden include some surprising statuary, such as sea-monsters with faces like Pekingese dogs. During the early 19th century dozens of live animals—not just dogs but lions and wolves—were boarded at Queluz, then the site of the royal zoo.

Queluz has one rather original attraction—an "artificial" river. Enclosed between restraining walls covered in precious painted *azulejos*, a real stream was diverted to pass through palace grounds and dammed whenever royal residents wanted a boat ride.

If you time your visit right, you can stay for lunch in the royal kitchen, now a restaurant. With giant old utensils, a fireplace big enough for a crowd to walk into, and loads of atmosphere, the place is called, logically, Cozinha Velha—the old kitchen.

Most museums are closed on Mondays, but country palaces take Tuesdays off—and any other day visiting kings or heads of state are in residence.

Sintra

Now for a town worth raving about. Sintra (25 km. northwest of Lisbon) is the kind of place you visit for a day and yearn to return to forever. Up and down forested hillsides are palaces and stately homes and lovely vistas. Even the local jail is in a castle. If you climb high enough in this up-and-down setting you can see as far as the sea. But the climbing, and

The climate may be Mediterranean but the sea is refreshingly Atlantic.

the distance between palaces, means only the very hardy will try to explore on foot.

Start right in the centre of town at **Paço da Vila** (the Royal Palace). Except for its two gi-

gantic, conical chimneys, this might at first glance seem like a fairly routine hulk of a palace. But don't judge by its some-what sombre façade. A summer home for Portuguese kings since the 14th century, the pal-ace's architecture became more and more unpredictable as wings were added over the **65** centuries with medieval and Manueline styles back-to-back. But the interiors and furnishings are exquisite. Among other treasures, this palace contains some of the oldest and most valuable *azulejos* in Portugal.

Every room of the Royal Palace has a story. For instance: once upon a time (17th century) Portugal had a dull-witted king named Afonso VI. He was pressured into abdicating for the good of the country, and his more effective brother, Pedro II, became king. When a plot to restore Afonso to the throne was discovered, the former monarch was exiled to Sintra. For nine years, until he died in 1683, he was imprisoned in a simple room of the Royal Palace. You can see the two paths his pacing wore in the brick floor.

A big, cheery hall of the palace tells a less tragic story. King João I (1385–1433) was caught in the act of kissing one of Queen Philippa's ladies-in-waiting. The king's far-fetched alibi was that the embrace was *"por bem"* (all to the good), perhaps hinting that top-secret affairs of state were involved. Palace gossips had a field day until the king ordered this ceiling painted with magpies—as many as there were ladies-in-waiting —their mouths sealed with the motto *"por bem"*.

Several other ceilings are worth craning your neck for. One is decorated with pictures of swans, each in a different

In Sintra, a town of captivating charm, typical azulejos *turn a wall fountain into a work of art.*

position. Another features the crests of noble families. And there are precious ceilings of intricate designs in the *mudéjar* style influenced by Moorish art.

As for those strange chimneys, shaped like upside-down ice-cream cones, they let the smoke out of the kitchen when oxen were being roasted for a couple of hundred visiting dignitaries.

Sintra's oldest monument, the **Castelo dos Mouros** (Moorish Castle), hugs a rocky hilltop overlooking the town. It was probably built in the 8th or 9th century, soon after the Moors occupied Portugal. The daunt-

less Afonso Henriques won it for the Christians in 1147—a major victory in the reconquest of Portugal. Now the castle is just a ruin, its crenellated walls still severe but with nothing behind to protect.

On a slightly higher hilltop, more than 1,500 feet above sea-level, stands the **Palácio da Pena,** a tremendous Victorian folly. To get there you drive through a park so lush with flowering trees and vines it seems like a tropical rain-forest.

In 1511 King Manuel I ordered a monastery built on this site. It was mostly destroyed in the earthquake of 1755, though a notable chapel and cloister survive. The present cocktail of Gothic, Renaissance, Manueline and Moorish architecture was designed as a love-nest for Queen Maria II (1834–53) and her romantic husband Ferdinand of Saxe-Coburg-Gotha. Few of us have the millions to indulge our fantasies so grandly. The **view** from the terrace of this Disneysque establishment sweeps all the way from the Atlantic to Lisbon.

Visit Sintra any day but

Tuesday, when the palaces are closed. If you can, go there on the second or fourth Sunday of the month, when a real country fair takes place in the adjacent village of SÃO PEDRO DE SINTRA. In this engrossing open market you can buy homemade bread, cheese and sausages, or a bottle of patent

Tourists pose for souvenir photo at mountaintop Palácio da Pena; right: market day in Alcobaça.

medicine sold by an old-fashioned, slick-talking hawker. Antique collectors find many possibilities here in rustic furniture, religious statues, old wagon wheels and 19th-century household appliances.

A final counsel: don't leave Sintra without buying a packet of *queijadas*, miniature cheesecakes in paper-thin crusts. These unique pastries may be the most delicate little cakes you'll come across anywhere in this sweet-toothed country.

Mafra

In modest Portugal the dimensions of the convent and palace of Mafra (40 km. north-west of Lisbon) are staggering. The frontage of this building, often likened to Spain's Escorial, measures more than 700 feet. Somebody has gone to the trouble of counting the pal-

Tidy fishing town of Ericeira improves defences against Atlantic.

ace's 4,500 windows and doors.

Blame the monumental extravagance on King João V. In 1711 he conceived this project to celebrate both his religious fervour and the seemingly endless shipments of gold arriving from Brazil. The king hired a German architect with Italian experience named Ludwig or Ludovice to take charge. The project gave work to as many as 50,000 artists, artisans and labourers.

On the trip from Lisbon you'll see ordinary country houses decorated—walls, steps and patios—with mosaics of marble chips. This is marble country, which helps to explain the liberal use of it in the **basilica** of the Mafra complex. Original effects are achieved by contrasting white marble columns, say with reddish marble walls. The statues are noteworthy, too.

The convent library has a vaulted ceiling and shelves housing 30,000 books.

The convent **hospital** is a bizarre church with 16 private sick-rooms along the nave so that patients could hear mass from their beds. If you're squeamish, skip the old pharmacy: along with perfectly charming apothecary jars, there is a gruesome display of some rather primitive medical tools.

With luck you may arrive in Mafra on the day of a carillon concert. The tone of the great bells is much admired, and they can be heard and enjoyed for miles around.

Most excursions go on another 8 or 10 kilometres to the coast for lunch at the fishing village of **Ericeira.** This is a winsome town of cobbled streets winding between whitewashed cottages, everything clean and neat and clearly treasured both by the inhabitants and Portuguese summer visitors. Lunch overlooking the Atlantic is bound to be entertaining, more so if you order the local seafood.

Ericeira received its town charter 750 years ago but scarcely attracted any attention until 1910, when Portugal's last king, Manuel II, hastily arrived from Mafra. In its little port, the king and his family boarded the royal yacht and sailed off to exile.

Arrábida Peninsula

It's only 32 kilometres south from Lisbon over the bridge to the calm, clean seashore at **Sesimbra.** This is a working fishing town. In the morning the entire adult male population seems to be occupied on or near the beach, taking the knots out of the tough plastic fishing lines. The beach is narrow but quite long, sheltered from the brunt of Atlantic tides and winds. And the golden sand is said to have a high iodine content—if you're impressed by things like this. Most of the tourist developments are designed to merge unobtrusively into the hillside.

Those **castle walls** silhouetted on the hilltop above Sesimbra are the genuine article, though recently restored. In the Middle Ages the whole town was situated up there, protected by the walls and the altitude. The Moors built the enclave, lost it to King Afonso Henriques in 1165, and won it back again for a few years, then had to move out for good in 1200.

Not much is left inside the walls but it's still worth the 6-kilometre ride up from present-day Sesimbra. First a small but ambitious archaeological museum has been set up in a room attached to the castle's 12th-century church. Second, the view looking down from the castle to the curve of the coast and back to the Arrábida mountains is splendid. And on the way up or down the hill you pass three squat white **windmills.** You may be surprised to learn that the country with the most windmills in Europe is Portugal (about 20,000 windmills, compared with less than 1,000 now in Holland).

Twelve kilometres southwest of Sesimbra is one of those end-of-the world promontories that must have been a sailors' nightmare. **Cabo Espichel,** the tip of the peninsula, attracts the most merciless Atlantic breakers. Just the place for a lighthouse, but it's also the unlikely setting for a sanctuary, Nossa Senhora do Cabo (Our Lady of the Cape). Pilgrims have been coming to this moody spot since the Middle Ages. The arcaded ensemble on either side of that lonely main square was built to house devout travellers. The church, dating from the end of the 17th century, stands at the very end of the line, high above the waves.

The topographical highlight of the Arrábida peninsula is a 35-kilometre-long mountain chain, the Serra da Arrábida, which protects the coast from the north winds and accounts

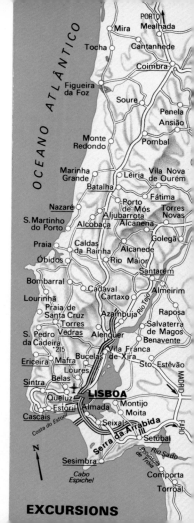

EXCURSIONS

for the Mediterranean vegetation.

Setúbal, the district capital, is an easy 40-kilometre drive from Lisbon. The bus does it in an hour; or you can take the ferry across the Tagus and then the train—a total of an hour and a half. The train is likely to be such a lazy local service that the conductor has time to shake hands with every small-town station-master along the route. By road or rail you'll admire the olive and citrus country with cows grazing among the

In timeless Portugal, donkeys and windmills still stand, and porters balance fish crates on padded hats.

trees—not at all the desolate terrain one associates with olives. The farther south you go, the more significant the vineyards. The Setúbal region produces a highly regarded muscatel.

Setúbal is a conglomeration of market town, resort centre and Portugal's third largest fishing port. Narrow, inviting shopping streets twist through the centre of the city; elsewhere there are more parks, squares, statues and monuments than a town of this size would normally boast.

Setúbal's greatest historical and artistic treasure, the **Igreja de Jesus,** was built about 1490

by the French architect Boy-tac—who later created Lisbon's glorious Jerónimos monastery. A dramatic main portal leads into the church with two inspired elements of decoration: 17th-century *azulejos* on the walls and pillars which look like twisted strands of clay, somehow fragile-looking in spite of their solid diameter.

The monastery has now been converted into the town museum, a grab-bag of early Portuguese paintings, archaeological odds and ends and old furniture and tiles. The cloister was reconstructed after the 1755 earthquake, but excavation has revealed parts of the original patio.

The 16th-century **fort** above the town is now a government-sponsored *pousada* (inn) with a dreamy sweeping view. Down at the sea-front, don't miss the action in the fishermen's quarter when the brightly painted boats of all sizes return with the fish still wriggling.

Across the broad Sado river from Setúbal is a sand dune with beaches so expansive they couldn't stay secret forever. You could drive to the Tróia peninsula the long way around—well over 100 kilometres—or get there in five minutes on a hovercraft from Setúbal.

To the North

All the excursion firms offer a long day's outing covering four major sites north of Lisbon: the shrine of Fátima, two monasteries that capture the history and heart of Portugal, and the most unabashedly picturesque fishing town in the whole country, Nazaré. The 11-hour outing (with lunch and coffee-and-shopping breaks along the way) covers a lot of ground—much of it memorable.

Fátima, a hill town about 135 kilometres north of Lisbon, has a 20th-century neoclassical basilica facing a square said to be twice as big as St. Peter's in Rome. This is where, in 1917, three young shepherds saw a series of miraculous visions, climaxed by a solar phenomenon witnessed by thousands. Two of the children died soon after the inexplicable events; the third, Lucia, is a Carmelite nun in Coimbra. She was last seen at the 50th anniversary ceremonies at Fátima, attended by the pope and an estimated 2 million faithful from around the world.

Faithful, old and young, share deep emotions at famed Fátima shrine.

Pilgrimages are held on the 13th of every month with the most important observances on the 13th of May and October. But even on an ordinary weekday crowds of believers, some in wheelchairs, some kneeling in penitence, come to Fátima. In spite of the nearby picnic grounds, parking lots and dozens of religious souvenir shops most of the gaudy side effects of a world-famous attraction have been avoided.

Halfway between Fátima and the coast stands the many-turreted **Mosteiro da Batalha** (Monastery of the Battle) consecrated to Santa Maria da Vitória. King João I ordered the construction of this Gothic masterpiece in gratitude for victory at nearby Aljubarrota in 1385. In the centre of the **Capela do Fundador** (Founder's Chapel), a tomb-for-two contains the remains of João and his queen, Philippa of Lancaster; their statues recline side by side and hand in hand. Niches in the walls hold the tombs of their children, most notably Henry the Navigator.

Still on a sepulchral note, Portugal's Unknown Soldiers are buried in the monastery's **Chapterhouse.** This vaulted chamber nearly 20 metres square was an engineering wonder in its day (around 1400). Because of fears that the unsupported ceiling would fall, the architect is said to have employed only convicts under sentence of death to work on the project.

The **Claustro Real** (Royal Cloister), like the church, began as a straightforward Gothic work but as construction continued a couple of centuries later the Manueline style imposed. Thus the columns and arches are decorated with the most unrestrained fantasies in filigreed stonework. By contrast, the carefully clipped hedges in the centre of the cloister are regimented in geometric patterns.

Older and bigger than Batalha is the former Cistercian monastery (Abadia Real de Santa Maria) at Alcobaça. This, too, was built to celebrate a victory—the 1147 battle in which King Afonso I took the town of Santarém from the Moors. Though the exterior of the church has suffered centuries of architectural tinkering the overall effect is harmonious. The interior of unadorned limestone is impressive; this is the biggest church in Portugal.

Elegant architecture of Alcobaça cloister encloses historic tombs.

In the transept, about 35 yards apart, are the **tombs** of King Pedro I and his beloved, Inês de Castro. The tombs are decorated with Portugal's greatest medieval stonecarving, telling the story of this romantic couple. Inês was murdered for political reasons in 1355, after having lived with Prince Pedro for ten happy years. When he became king two years later, Pedro exhumed her body, crowned it, and ordered all the nobles to kneel and kiss the skeleton's hand.

For a bit of relief from this tragic love story, be sure to visit the 18th-century kitchens with their monumental tiled fireplaces. River water was channelled directly into the kitchen, so the monks could fill their tea-kettles and catch their dinner at the same time.

Nazaré, Portuguese for Nazareth, is that fishing village you've seen in pictures. And everything is true: the fishermen do wear black stocking-caps and plaid trousers; oxen sometimes pull the wide, flat-bottomed boats ashore (though tractors are now more common). And the women really wear bright aprons and seven petticoats.

Sítio, the 300-foot cliff at the north end of Nazaré, is a supreme vantage point over the

green hilly countryside, the tile roofs of the neatly packed town, and mile after mile of **beach** open to the full force of the Atlantic. The scene is a bit of a shock in summer, though, when thousands of tents fill the beaches, providing some shade for sunburned vacationers. Nazaré is in the big-time tourism

business but the fishing and folklore seem unaffected. On the straight but narrow streets the whitewashed houses are as charming as the way the girls walk, flouncing all their skirts.

Two nagging Nazaré questions. First, why do they wear seven petticoats? Some say for the days of the week, but the

To fetch a pail of water, women of Nazaré climb to the local fountain.

answer is lost in legend. Second, how can you confirm that they wear exactly seven petticoats? Easy: count them—at any local souvenir shop on the costumed dolls.

What to Do

Shopping

Lisbon is a sophisticated capital city where you still see women walking with heavy baskets or bundles balanced on their heads. The shopping also runs to extremes—from chic boutiques to outdoor markets. You can buy cheap trinkets (some remarkably attractive) or expensive works of gold or silver. Between the cheapest and the dearest you're likely to find just what you were looking for.

When to Shop

The shops of Lisbon are open five-and-a-half days a week: Monday to Friday from 9 a.m. to 1 p.m. and 3 to 7 p.m. and on Saturday morning from 9 to 1. The "commercial centres", new shopping complexes, usually operate from 10 a.m. to midnight or even later, often on Sundays as well. The Lisbon flea market, at Campo de Santa Clara, runs Tuesdays and Saturdays all day. The vast country market at São Pedro de Sintra is held the second and fourth Sunday of each month. Note: haggling may be appropriate at antique stalls in the flea market but nowhere else.

What to Buy

Handicrafts excel in Portugal, but where to start? Here are some ideas in alphabetical order.

Antiques. The line between precious relics and old-fashioned junk is always narrow, but knowledgeable collectors will want to browse around the shops in Rua Dom Pedro V— the busy street descending from the Rato to Cais do Sodré. If it's nostalgia you're after, the flea markets are gold mines of ancient typewriters, rusty roller-skates and retired Portuguese army boots. For the rustic touch, you may pick up such quaint country relics as used cowbells, pitchforks and wagon wheels at village markets.

Baskets. Each region has its own way of weaving willow or rushes or straw into baskets for farm or home. They're strong, useful and often pretty. Bonus: no overweight baggage problem.

Capes. In the Alentejo region, south of Lisbon, they wear long cloaks in winter, usually brown, with fur collars. Miniature models are delightful for children. You can also

From egg cups and spice cabinets to bowls and platters, Portuguese woodwork has many kitchen uses.

find traditional flowing capes, just the thing for a princess.

Copperware. Charming toy-sized pots and pans as well as conventional utensils, coffee sets and bric-à-brac.

Cork. Portugal is the world's leading producer, and not only to stopper those millions of wine bottles. You'll find decorative spin-offs—intricate cork sculptures, for instance, and lightweight knick-knacks.

Dolls. In the authentic costumes of the regions of Portugal.

Embroidery. Thousands of women on the island of Madeira produce delicate needlework that is known worldwide.

The linen or organdy table-cloths are admirable but expensive. Though you can surely afford a handkerchief. Hand embroidery also comes from those other Portuguese islands, the Azores, and some mainland villages, notably Viana do Castelo. And look for intricate lace-work from towns all along the Portuguese coast.

Filigree. When the Moors invaded Iberia in the 8th century they brought this style of art with them; it's still going strong. The most unmistakably Portuguese design is a caravel confected of gold or silver wire. The same craftsmen also produce brooches in the form of flowers or butterflies.

Hand-painted miscellany. Paperweights, ashtrays, candle-sticks and other economical mementos, usually in happy colours.

Ironwork. Though heavy going on the baggage scales, the old-fashioned lamps, flower-pot-holders, etc. of wrought iron are certainly worth looking at.

Knitwear. Hand-knit pull-overs in sophisticated designs or rugged fishermen's sweaters.

Leather. You may find a bargain in a belt, a bag or a pair of shoes.

Macao imports. Portugal's Chinese connection still supplies change-of-pace shopping ideas: genuine oriental tea sets, rice bowls... even furniture.

Madeira wine. Take home a bottle or two of this celebrated product of the sunny island's volcanic soil. May be served before or after dinner, depending on which variety you choose.

Oil paintings. Portuguese artists paint in varied styles but most tourists like pictures of places to remember. Fishing boats and seafaring folk are favourite themes, along with the twisting streets of Alfama.

Port. The legendary wine from the Douro Valley near Oporto is best known as an after-dinner tradition but also comes in aperitif versions. Even in Portugal really good port can be an expensive hobby.

Pottery. A long, distinguished but slightly mixed-up history starting with the Phoenicians accounts for the many different designs and objects in Portuguese porcelain. Look for fine workmanship and cheerful colours.

Records. So you can take the haunting lament of the *fado* back home with you.

Some handcrafted gift suggestions: flowered embroidery from Cascais and pottery from the Alentejo.

Roosters. Statuettes of ceramic or wood, brightly hand-painted, honouring the rooster which arose from the judge's dinner plate and crowed to proclaim the innocence of an unjustly condemned man... as the story goes in the northern town of Barcelos, where they make the figurines.

Rugs. Look for the ones from Arraiolos, an Alentejo village with a three-century-old rug industry. Bright colours and equally cheerful designs.

Shawls. If the sweeping black model affected by *fado* singers isn't the "real you", look into the selection of gaily designed scarves.

Tiles. Hand-painted *azulejos* have been decorating Portuguese walls for centuries. You can buy a single blue-and-white tile square or a batch to assemble into a large picture when you get home. Some places will paint tiles to order if your patio needs a special effect.

Wickerwork. Aside from baskets you'll also find hand-made wicker chairs and tables, ship models and animal figures.

Yokes. Oxen used them first, but now people have discovered that they make charmingly rustic head-boards or chair-backs. Nicely carved scale models serve as hat-racks.

Sports

From the simplest pursuits—swimming and hiking—to the complexities of deep-sea fishing, sports enthusiasts can usually find what they're looking for in the Lisbon area. The gentle climate means year-round golf and tennis.

Water Activities

Swimming. The government tourist office issues a leaflet on Portuguese beaches, with maps and details of facilities. Eight of the major beaches belong to what's called the Lisbon Coast, from Guincho to the suburbs of Setúbal. Though Estoril is the best known internationally, several others in the region are at least equally appealing. An immense stretch of open beach on the Tróia peninsula may be reached from Setúbal by hovercraft.

Undersea sports. The extraordinarily clear, calm waters off Sesimbra favour all snorkelling and scuba activity.

Water-ski. Estoril and Portinho da Arrábida (between Sesimbra and Setúbal).

Sailing and boating. Most beaches which are protected from the open ocean have rowing-boats, canoes or pedalos for rent by the hour. Experienced sailors in search of more seaworthy craft can ask at the local yacht or sailing club.

Fishing. All along the coast you'll see anglers in boots casting from the beaches, others perched on rocks or man-made promontories. They mostly say business is good. The area's best deep-sea fishing is around Sesimbra where the game is swordfish.

Sports Ashore

Golf. The Lisbon area has two major 18-hole courses—the Estoril Golf Club and, south of the Tagus, the Lisbon Country Club. The Lisbon Sports Club's 14-hole course is 20 kilometres northwest of the capital in Belas. Estoril Sol is a new nine-hole course.

Tennis. Major hotels have their own courts, but there are tennis clubs and public courts as well.

Riding. You can hire a horse, with or without an instructor, at the Lisbon Country Club or at one of several riding academies in and around Lisbon.

Spectator sports

Football (soccer). As in most countries, this draws big crowds in Portugal. Lisbon's two major teams are the rivals Benfica and Sporting.

Horse-racing. Since the 14th-century the government has regulated horse-breeding in Portugal, so it's only right that racing (at Campo Grande hippodrome) is popular.

Horse shows. Riding and jumping competitions are held in Cascais.

Car racing. At Estoril's autodrome, on the road to Sintra.

Festivals

Portugal's folk festivals are too modest to be classed with such international attractions as the Carnival in Rio or the running of the bulls in Pamplona. But if you happen to be in Portugal during one of the celebrations, so much the better. The tourist information office in central Lisbon posts a timetable of festivals and fairs around the country, which is worth checking as you plan your excursions.

Most of the colourful religious processions are confined to the north of the country. In the towns around Lisbon the Patron Saint's Day may be celebrated both at church and with dancing in the streets, fire-works and bullfights.

Carnival in Lisbon is a rather subdued affair. Firecrackers go off in the streets, but the pre-Lenten festivities tend to be confined to private parties.

June is the month of Lisbon's "popular saints"—Anthony, John and Peter. Fairs are held in the neighbourhoods with folkdancing, sports compe-

Solemnity of festival near Batalha can't quell young participant's grin.

titions and firework displays. The biggest day is June 13, honouring the local lad who grew up to be St. Anthony of Padua (see p. 35).

Bullfights

Children over six are admitted to Portuguese bullfights. You should have no qualms about taking your own tots to see all the colour and drama of the *corrida* without the killing. The fights are less conclusive than the classic Spanish version— but probably more fun.

At a typical *corrida* eight bulls, each weighing nearly half a ton, will enter the arena in turn. Four are fought *à antiga portuguesa*, in the uniquely Portuguese way. And four are taken on by a matador who doesn't kill but dominates the bull with his cape. Lacking picadors and the "moment of truth", this is a rather tame variant of the Spanish bullfight.

But the four rounds *à antiga*, containing elements of a circus, a horse-show and a rodeo, can be memorably exciting. The horses, with ribbons in their manes, are fearless, high-stepping, loyal and agile. The bullfighters, dressed in dashing period costumes with breeches, maintain superb control over their mounts. Horse and rider are as one, teamed to arouse the bull, outrun and outwit him. During each chase the *cavalheiro* (horseman) stabs a long dart into the bull's shoulder. When the quota of darts *(farpas)* have been inserted, the horseman salutes the crowd with his three-cornered hat and leaves the field.

The second act of each fight *à antiga* abandons elegance in favour of reckless rough-house. Eight very brave young men leap over the fence onto the sand to face the bull on foot, ostentatiously unarmed. Fortunately the bull's horns have been padded, but he can still do damage to anybody in his way. The men on foot *(forcados)* subdue the bull with their bare hands. Or try to.

Lisbon's Campo Pequeno bullring is a Victorian red-brick landmark with mock Moorish arches and grotesque bulbous domes. The arena in Cascais is bigger, but a bullfighter hasn't "arrived" until he's won the esteem of the finicky fans at Campo Pequeno. The season runs from Easter Sunday to October. As in Spain, seats in the shade *(sombra)* cost more than in the sun *(sol)*, though there are night performances as well. For a modicum of comfort, rent a pillow from the usher.

Nightlife

Even if you're not usually the nightclub type, make an exception in Lisbon. You can have a rousing night out at one of the *fado* houses in Alfama or the Bairro Alto, an experience you can't find anywhere else. And though a century ago "respectable" people were reluctant to be seen in a *fado* club, nowadays there's no danger at all—physically, morally or financially.

A learned monograph on the *fado* warns that it should not be sung in the daytime. This may be carrying things a bit far, but it's obvious that the dramatic atmosphere of a *fado* house adds to the impact. Guitarists on a little stage play a warm-up number. Then the lights dim, the audience quiets down, and a spotlight picks out a woman in black who wails out a song of tragedy and despair. Her sultry voice sums up that most Portuguese word, *saudade*—longing, regret, nostalgia. It can send a shiver down your spine.

Most *fado* singers are women, but you may also hear a man perform the same sort of ballad with a strong, husky voice and tragic mannerisms. The singer is usually accompanied by two guitars.

The *fado* is never danced—

it's much too solemn—but sometimes regional fishermen's and shepherd's dances enliven the show.

In Lisbon, you can also find conventional nightclubs with extravagant floor-shows and intimate *boîtes*, discotheques, jazz clubs and bars for all tastes.

Serious music. The lively Lisbon cultural scene offers opera, ballet, symphony concerts and recitals. The capital's opera company is highly regarded. The Gulbenkian Foundation maintains its own symphony orchestra and ballet company. Portugal has three other symphony orchestras and a national dance company. Soloists and ensembles from many countries also perform here. Check your hotel desk or the government tourist office to find out what's coming up.

Theatre and cinema. Most of Lisbon's stage plays are comedies and revues—in Portuguese, of course. Cinemas show foreign films in the original language with Portuguese subtitles. *Diário de Notícias* publishes the most complete stage and screen listings, including times of performances.

Gambling. If you don't know the rules of roulette, "French Bank", baccarat, craps or blackjack, the Estoril Casino helpfully issues illustrated instruction leaflets in English and Portuguese. And then you're on your own. But first you have to pay a fee and show your passport to enter the gaming rooms. The casino is open from 3 p.m. to 3 a.m. daily (except Good Friday and Christmas Eve). A sign outside "suggests" that gentlemen wear jackets after 8 p.m., but no

Life mirrors art as nightclub performers present the music of the fado.

rules are enforced. A tip on tipping: if you win, flip a chip or two to the croupier. All the gaming-room employees share the gratuities.

For less glamourous gambling, you could try your hand at the Portuguese football pools—Totobola—or the weekly national lottery.

Wining and Dining

The only problem in Portuguese restaurants is the size of the portions—simply gargantuan. With a little practice, though, you'll soon be coping —and perhaps even find room for dessert.

Seafood fans are in luck here, and if you've been unenthusiastic until now, the taste of just-caught fish and shellfish may be enough to convert you. Not that the local menus skimp on meat. You can find delicious pork and lamb dishes and even a presentable steak. You'll also enjoy the flavour of freshly picked fruits and vegetables. And the wines are eminently drinkable.

Choosing a Restaurant
Government inspectors rate all Portuguese restaurants on a scale of four categories. In descending order they are *de luxo* (luxury), *de primeira, de segunda* and *de terceira classe* (first, second and third class). The higher the ratings the more the restaurant is permitted to charge. A sign announcing the class is often affixed outside

---

* For more information on wining and dining in Portugal, consult the Berlitz EUROPEAN MENU READER.

restaurants; menus displayed in the window or just beside the door let you know what to expect in variety and price. Prices normally include taxes and a service charge, but you'll want to leave an additional 5 to 10 per cent tip for good service. Whether you live it up in the most elegant establishment or test the local colour in a humble fishermen's hangout, the service will most likely be quick, attentive and helpful.

Meal Times
Breakfast *(o pequeno almoço)* is eaten anytime until about 10 a.m. Lunch *(o almoço)* is served from shortly after noon until 3 p.m. Dinner *(o jantar)* runs from 7.30 to 9.30 p.m., though later in a *casa de fado*. Between-meal snacks may be found at a *pastelaria* (pastry and cake shop) or *salão de chá* (tea shop), or what the Portuguese call a *snack-bar*.

Breakfast
Because lunch and dinner tend to be major productions, you may prefer the kind of light breakfast the Portuguese eat: coffee, toast or rolls, butter and jam. Hotels can provide all the extras—juice, eggs, bacon or whatever else is required to duplicate an English or American breakfast.

Soups
Lunch and dinner often get off to a hearty start:

Caldo verde (green soup) is the most distinctive Portuguese soup—a thick broth of potato purée and finely-shredded cabbage or kale. Sometimes a bit of sausage is added.

Sopa à Portuguesa is similar, but with added beans, broccoli, carrots, turnips and anything else the cook happened to think of.

Sopa de cozido: a very rich meat broth with cabbage and perhaps macaroni added. (This is often followed by *cozido*—a huge serving of all the things that were boiled to create the broth, including beef, pork, chicken, sausages, potatoes, cabbage and carrots.)

Don't confuse *sopa de grão* (chick-pea) with *sopa de agrião* (cream of watercress).

Canja de galinha is chicken and rice soup.

Note: Portuguese cooks are so confident of their seasoning that salt and pepper are seldom put on the dinner table. But you can have them for the asking —"*sal e pimenta, por favor*"— and the chef won't sulk.

From the Deep
The best advertisement is in the window of a restaurant—a refrigerated display case full of

prawns and crabs, oysters and mussels, sea-bass and sole. Seafood restaurants generally sell shellfish by weight, giving the price in escudos per kilo.

Some unusual ideas:

Ameijoas na cataplana: an invention from the Algarve, steamed mussels (clams) with sausages, ham, white wine, tomato, onion and herbs.

Açorda de marisco: a spicy, garlic-scented bread-soup full of seafood bits; raw eggs are folded into the mixture at the table.

Lulas recheadas: tender squid stuffed with rice, olives, herbs, onion and tomato.

Lampreia à Minho: a bed of rice and a red wine sauce beautify this unlovely lamprey, quite a delicacy in Portugal.

Bacalhau: Cod is the national dish of Portugal, even though it comes dried and salted and expensively from distant seas; odd because some of the tastiest fresh fish in the world is right on the "doorstep". Depending on which fishwife's tale you believe, cod is served in 100, 365 or 1,000 different ways. Flaky, meaty chunks are baked with parsley, potatoes, onion and olives and garnished with grated hardboiled egg under the name *Bacalhau à Gomes de Sá.*

Fresh fish, whole or filleted, is usually served grilled, as are outstanding *atum*, tunny (tuna) and *espadarte*, swordfish steaks. The Portuguese are fond of boiled fish dishes served with cabbage and boiled potatoes —doused with oil and vinegar.

Meat

Bife na frigideira: not what you think it is. *Frigideira* means frying pan, and this dish is a beefsteak nicely done in a wine sauce.

Cabrito assado: baked kid served with potato and rice, heavy going but delicious.

Carne de porco à Alentejana: an inspired idea, pork in a clam-sauce.

Espetada mista: a Portuguese shish-kebab—chunks of beef, lamb and pork on a spit.

Feijoada: a far cry from the more elaborate national dish of Brazil, but still a filling stew of pigs' feet and sausage, white beans and cabbage.

Many dishes are served with *both* rice and potatoes.

And a warning here that Portuguese menus are often unintentionally misleading when foreign names are used. Fanciful chefs dub favourite recipes "à provençal" or "à Yorkshire" or whatever else sounds exotic. But the dish may have no connection at all with the usual gastronomic interpretation.

Game and Fowl

Chicken—*frango* or *galinha*—is popular cooked in many ways: stewed in wine sauce, fried, roast and barbecued to a tasty crisp.

Some restaurants specialize in game—*codorniz* (quail), *perdiz* (partridge), *lebre* (hare) and even *javali* (wild boar).

Dessert

The national sweet-tooth may be too much for your taste. Where else do people pour sugar on a sliced sweet orange? But the cakes, custards and pastries—usually involving egg yolks—are really delicious.

Pudim flã—sometimes written *flam* or *flan* or *flão*—is the Portuguese version of Spanish *flan* (caramel custard).

Arroz doce: rice pudding with a dash of cinnamon.

Maçã assada: sugary baked apple.

Pudim Molotov: nobody's certain about the derivation of the name, but it's surely the richest dessert to explode any diet. Fluffy eggwhite mousse immersed in caramel sauce.

All of which may deflect you toward cheese. The richest

and most expensive in Portugal is *Serra da Estrela*, a cured ewe's-milk cheese from the country's highest mountain range. It's creamy and soft with a delicate flavour. Another cheese on many menus, *Flamengo* resembles Gouda. Some restaurants serve something called *queijo fresco* as an

Baker wraps up queijadas, *delicate little cheese pies native to Sintra.*

appetizer, even before you've been handed the menu. This small white, soft mini-cheese made of ewe's and goat's milk is so bland you'll want to add pepper and salt.

Change of Pace
Thanks to Portugal's imperial memories you can experiment with a little known, delicious type of food while you're in Lisbon. The former colony of Goa accounts for the popularity of *caril* (curry) and other Indian-style dishes among the Portuguese. A typical Goan delicacy, less pungent than Indian food, is *xacuti* (pronounced and sometimes spelled *chacuti*). It's simply chunks of fried chicken in a sauce of pepper, coriander, cumin, cloves, cinnamon, anise, saffron and coconut milk, served with steamed rice.

Another colonial heritage links Lisbon with the territory of Macao, assuring lovers of Chinese food a night out with *gambas doces* (sweet and sour prawns) and all the fixings.

Table Wines
Portugal is one of those fortunate countries where all you really need to tell the waiter is *tinto* (red) or *branco* (white) and you can't go wrong. The house wine in any restaurant is

potable; some are admirable. And if the choice of red or white isn't broad enough, you can order pink or green.

Vinho verde ("green wine"), from the north-west, is Portugal's most distinctive wine. It's really a young white wine, semi-sparkling and thoroughly delightful. A less well-known variant is red wine from the same region, bearing the improbable name *vinho verde tinto* ("red green wine"). Both types should be served chilled.

So should Portuguese rosé, which is also slightly bubbly and may be either sweet or very dry.

Vinho espumante, usually sweet and full of froth, is the Portuguese sparkling wine packaged suggestively in a Champagne-shaped bottle.

There are several wine-producing regions near Lisbon with names controlled by law. You may come across these classifications:

Bucelas—light, fresh white wine

Colares—light red wine of tradition

Setúbal—mellow sweet white, sometimes served as an aperitif.

A major region in northern Portugal is Dão, producing vigorous reds and flavourful whites.

Other Drinks

The two most celebrated Portuguese wines, port and Madeira are mostly known as dessert wines, but they may also be sipped as aperitifs. The before-dinner varieties are dry or extra-dry white port and the dry Madeiras, *Sercial* and *Verdelho*. They should be served slightly chilled. After dinner, sip one of the famous ruby or tawny ports, or a Madeira dessert wine, *Boal* and *Malvasia* (Malmsey).

Portuguese beers are good. Light or dark, they are usually served chilled, bottled or from the tap.

You can find various brands of mineral water in small or large bottles, bubbly or still.

Portuguese fruit juices are delicious. Well-known soft drinks are also available.

Adventurous drinkers may want to investigate *aguardente*, a powerful brandy.

Coffee

At the end of lunch or dinner most people order a *bica*, a small cup of black espresso coffee. Curiously, a diluted black coffee is called a *carioca*—even though the Cariocas (inhabitants of Rio de Janeiro) drink theirs infinitely stronger. Cafés also serve white coffee; in a tall glass it's called a *galão*.

Tea *(chá)* is very popular. After all, the Portuguese explorers introduced it to the western world.

To Help You Order . . .

Could we have a table?
Do you have a set-price menu?

Queríamos uma mesa.
Tem uma ementa turística?

I'd like a/an/some . . .

Queria . . .

beer	**uma cerveja**	milk	**leite**
bill	**conta**	mineral water	**água mineral**
bread	**pão**	napkin	**um guardanapo**
butter	**manteiga**	potatoes	**batatas**
coffee	**um café**	rice	**arroz**
dessert	**uma sobremesa**	salad	**uma salada**
fish	**peixe**	sandwich	**uma sanduíche**
fruit	**fruta**	soup	**uma sopa**
ice-cream	**um gelado**	sugar	**açúcar**
meat	**carne**	tea	**chá**
menu	**a ementa**	wine	**vinho**

99

... and Read the Menu

alho	garlic	**gambas**	prawns (shrimp)
almôndegas	meatballs	**gelado**	ice-cream
alperces	apricots	**guisado**	stew
ameijoas	baby clams	**lagosta**	spiny lobster
ananaz	pineapple	**laranja**	orange
arroz	rice	**legumes**	vegetables
assado	roast	**limão**	lemon
atum	tunny (tuna)	**linguado**	sole
azeitonas	olives	**lombo**	loin
bacalhau	codfish	**lulas**	squid
banana	banana	**(à sevilhana)**	(deep-fried)
besugo	sea bream	**maçã**	apple
bife (vaca)	beef steak	**mariscos**	shellfish
biscoitos/	biscuits	**melancia**	watermelon
bolachas	(cookies)	**mexilhões**	mussels
bolo	cake	**molho**	sauce
borrego	lamb	**morangos**	strawberries
cabrito	kid	**omelete**	omelette
caracóis	snails	**ostras**	oysters
caranguejo	crab	**ovo**	egg
cavala	mackerel	**peixe**	fish
cebola	onion	**pescada**	hake
chouriço	a spicy	**pescadinha**	whiting
	sausage	**pêssego**	peach
coelho	rabbit	**pimento**	green pepper
cogumelos	mushrooms	**polvos**	baby octopus
costeletas	chops	**pequenos**	
couve	cabbage	**porco**	pork
dobrada	tripe	**presunto**	ham
dourada	sea-bass	**queijo**	smoked cheese
enguias	eel	**romãs**	pomegranates
ervilhas	peas	**salmonete**	red mullet
feijões	beans	**salsichão**	salami
filete	fillet	**sardinhas**	sardines
flã	caramel	**sobremesa**	dessert
	mould	**torrada**	toast
framboesas	raspberries	**truta**	trout
frango	chicken	**uvas**	grapes
frito	fried	**vitela**	veal

How to Get There

From North America

BY AIR: Lisbon is linked with New York, Montreal and Detroit on a daily basis, and on certain days of the week you can fly direct from Atlanta, Boston, Houston, St. Louis and Toronto. There are also daily connecting flights from more than 50 American cities and about a dozen major Canadian cities.

Visitors to Lisbon may take advantage of two reduced-rate fares. Excursion fares, good for trips lasting 14 to 60 days, may be purchased any time before departure and no cancellation fees are imposed. These fares change for high and low season and are subject to weekend surcharges.

The 14- to 60-day APEX (Advance Purchase Excursion) fare must be booked and the ticket purchased 21 days prior to departure. All arrangements for the new 7- to 60-day Super-APEX fare must be completed 30 days before departure. APEX fares are subject to cancellation fees.

Charter Flights and Package Tours: One- to three-week tours are now being offered to Lisbon in combination with Madeira, the Canary Islands, the Azores, the Algarve, as well as major cities in Spain. These GIT (Group-Inclusive Tour) charters feature round-trip air transport, hotel, transfers, some sightseeing and meals and are available to groups of five or more. Your travel agent can also make arrangements for optional "Dine Around" plans and for car rental service. When making your plans, check with a reliable agent for any ABC (Advance Booking Charters, only air transport) or OTC (One Stop Inclusive Tour Charters) available.

From the United Kingdom

BY AIR: Scheduled flights leave London (Gatwick) daily, and connections are made there from other parts of Great Britain. The types of fare available are first class and excursion (for stays of more than five days). There are special fares your travel agent can arrange if you are travelling alone, with one other person (and staying for a specific number of weeks) or with a group. There are discounts for spouse, students, young people, school groups and common interest groups.

A wide variety of package tours are available to Lisbon, including one with a basic (charter) air fare plus a nominal charge for accommodation that you find for yourself; others offer fly/drive arrangements, art treasure tours and air/coach tours taking in Spain and Morocco.

BY ROAD: The Calais ferry crossing is the quickest if you are driving to Lisbon. Although the Weymouth-Cherbourg crossing would save some driving time, it takes longer as a whole. You can also cross from Dover to Boulogne or Calais by hovercraft. This is faster than the ferry and can be cheaper. You are advised to book your crossing early.

From Calais there are toll motorways most of the way to Lisbon, or you might find a more pleasant drive on secondary roads via Bordeaux, Bilbao or Zaragoza, Madrid and then across to Lisbon. You can put your car on a train (at some expense) either from Boulogne to the south of France or from Paris to Lisbon.

BY RAIL: There's daily rail service from Paris to Lisbon; you could catch a Paris-bound train from London, and once on the Continent take advantage of the Inter-Rail pass—a flat-rate unlimited mileage ticket good for visitors under 26 or over 65—or other economical tickets. The journey from Paris takes about 24 hours, with sleepers and couchettes available.

BY SEA: Although there are no direct passenger services to Lisbon, there are a large number of cruises to choose from that stop there en route.

When to Go

In spite of a relatively stable year-round temperature in Portugal, Lisbon has an Atlantic climate influenced by the Mediterranean, which offers mild winters even if there's a good chance of rain. Spring and autumn are the best seasons to be in Lisbon, although you can take advantage of the summer sun at the beaches.

Following are the average monthly temperatures in Lisbon:

	J	F	M	A	M	J	J	A	S	O	N	D
°F	52	54	57	61	64	70	73	73	72	66	59	54
°C	11	12	14	16	18	21	23	23	22	19	15	12

Sea temperatures at Estoril:

	J	F	M	A	M	J	J	A	S	O	N	D
°F	55	55	57	59	60	63	63	63	63	63	61	57
°C	13	13	14	15	16	17	17	17	17	17	16	14

Planning Your Budget

To give you an idea of what to expect, here are some average prices in Portuguese escudos. However, remember that all prices must be regarded as approximate and that inflation is running very high.

Airport: bus fare to Cais do Sodré 15 esc.; green double-decker bus to Santa Apolónia 40 esc.; taxi fare 160 esc. In taxis, a surcharge of 50% must be paid if luggage exceeds 20 kg.

Babysitters: 110 esc. per hour until 8 p.m.; 130 esc. per hour after 8 p.m.; 50% more on weekends.

Camping: 25 esc. per person, 25–35 esc. per tent, 12.50–15 esc. per car, 30–40 esc. per caravan.

Car hire: Morris Mini: 530 esc. per day, 3,640 esc. per week, plus 5.30 esc. per km.; Ford Escord: 690 esc. per day, 4,760 esc. per week, plus 8.60 esc. per km.; Mercedes 230: 2,310 esc. per day, 16,100 esc. per week, plus 20.30 esc. per km.

Cigarettes: foreign 80–100 esc., cheapest Portugese 30 esc. for 20.

Entertainment: bullfight 220–1,000 esc.; cinema 80–100 esc.; discotheque 500–1,500 esc.; fado 500 esc. minimum.

Guides, Interpreters: 1,000 esc. half day; 1,800 esc. 8-hour day.

Hairdressers, Barbers: men's razor cut 150–180 esc.; shave 25–60 esc.; haircut 90–100 esc.; women's haircut 200–500 esc.; shampoo and set 180–300 esc.; manicure 70–100 esc.; certain establishments charge far less.

Hotels average prices (double room with bath per night): ***** 2,000–4,000 esc., **** 1,920–2,600 esc., *** 1,000–1,500 esc., ** 850–1,400 esc., * 680–880 esc., boarding house 600–1,050 esc.

Laundry and dry cleaning: laundry (ironed): shirt/blouse 50–90 esc., pyjamas/nightgown 50–80 esc.; dry cleaning: sweater/blouse 160 esc., skirt/trousers 130–350 esc., sports jacket 160 esc., long dress 230–400 esc.

Meals and drinks: Continental breakfast 70 esc., lunch 250 esc., dinner 400 esc., coffee 10–30 esc., beer 15–40 esc., brandy (local) 50 esc., gin and tonic 100–140 esc., wine (bottle) 90–250 esc.

Public transport: Metro 10 esc., tourist pass for 1 week unlimited travel on Lisbon's public transport system (except on the Metro) 200 esc., otherwise bus and tram fares depend on distance travelled.

Taxis: typical metered fares: airport to Pombal 75 esc., Rossio to Gulbenkian Museum 50 esc., Restauradores to Belém 80 esc.

BLUEPRINT for a Perfect Trip

An A-Z Summary of Practical Information and Facts

Listed after most main entries is an appropriate Portuguese translation usually in the singular. You'll find this vocabulary useful when asking for information or assistance.

A

ACCOMMODATION—see **HOTELS, YOUTH HOSTELS**

AIRPORT *(aeroporto).* The Aeroporto de Lisboa (also known by the suburb where it's located, Portela) is only a 15-minute drive from the centre of Lisbon when traffic is light. Facilities for arriving passengers include a bank, car-rental desks and a tourist office as well as porters or free baggage trolleys. Departing passengers can do last-minute shopping at souvenir stands and the duty-free shop. There are also bars and a restaurant.

Besides taxis, which are plentiful (see Taxis), you can take buses number 44 or 45 for the Cais do Sodré station (abbreviated "C. Sodré") about every 15 minutes during the day and every 25 minutes in the early morning and late evening. They pass through the city centre, including the Rossio. From the Cais do Sodré station buses to the airport are marked "Moscavide" (44) and "Prior Velho" (45). Green double-decker buses link the airport with the Santa Apolónia station. For fares, see page 103.

For information on flight times call 80 20 60; the main airport number is 88 11 01.

Where do I get the bus to the airport/to the centre of Lisbon?

Onde posso apanhar o autocarro para o aeroporto/para o centro da cidade?

BABYSITTERS *(babysitter)*. Tourists can reserve a babysitter at the Hospedeiras de Portugal (tel. 60 43 53) or another of the commercial services listed under "babysitters" in the yellow pages directory. You must book by 6 p.m. for the same evening, but to be sure of having a sitter you should call the day before. For weekends, arrangements must be made by 6 p.m. on Friday. Your hotel can also help you find a sitter.

Can you get me a babysitter for tonight?	**Pode encontrar-me uma babysitter para esta noite?**

BANKS and CURRENCY EXCHANGE *(banco; câmbio)*. Currency exchange is carried out exclusively by banks in Portugal; in tourist areas some remain open later and on weekends to change money. Normal banking hours are from 9 a.m. to noon and 2 to 3.30 p.m., Mondays to Fridays. At the airport you'll find an exchange office which operates until 11 p.m.; the exchange office *(câmbio)* at the Santa Apolónia railway station stays open from 9 a.m. to 9 p.m. and one bank in Praça dos Restauradores is open from 6 p.m. to 11 p.m. for the benefit of tourists. Be sure to take along your passport when cashing traveller's cheques.

I want to change some pounds/dollars.	**Queria trocar libras/dólares.**
Can you cash a traveller's cheque?	**Pode pagar um cheque de viagem?**

BARBERS'—see **HAIRDRESSERS'**

BUSES—see **PUBLIC TRANSPORT**

CAMPING. Portugal has around 70 camping sites, mostly near beaches or historic monuments. Several are in the Lisbon area, such as the Monsanto Park site, a delightful forest within the city limits. Facilities range from the most simple to the most elaborate (with swimming pools, tennis courts, bars and restaurants).

To stay in the organized camping spots you must show your passport and in certain sites you must have an official card identifying you as a member of a national or international camping association. Outside of recognized sites you must not camp within city limits or on beaches and other public places, nor light fires in forests. You should leave your site clean by burying any litter.

Information on camping can be obtained from the tourist office, which has an excellent brochure, or the Federação Portuguesa de Campismo, Rua Voz do Operário 1, 1000-Lisboa, tel. 86 23 50.

May we camp here?	**Podemos acampar aqui?**
We have a caravan (trailer).	**Nós temos uma roulotte.**

CAR HIRE (*carros de aluguer*). International and local car-hire firms operate in Lisbon and major tourist areas. The minimum age for hiring a car is generally 25, and you must have a valid licence held for at least one year. If you present a recognized credit card the deposit will be waived. Third-party insurance is included in the basic charge but a collision-damage waiver and personal accident policy may be added (see PLANNING YOUR BUDGET, page 103).

I'd like to hire a car today/tomorrow.	**Queria alugar um carro para hoje/amanhã.**
for one day/a week	**por um dia/uma semana**
Please include full insurance.	**Que inclua um seguro contra todos os riscos, por favor.**

CHEMISTS'—see **MEDICAL CARE**

CIGARETTES, CIGARS, TOBACCO (*cigarros, charutos, tabaco*). Cigarettes imported from Europe and the United States cost about three times as much as similar Portuguese brands. Among popular local makes: SG, Ritz, Porto. For prices see PLANNING YOUR BUDGET on page 103.

Tobacco shops also sell an ample range of Portuguese and imported cigars and pipe tobacco.

Smoking is prohibited in theatres and cinemas, indoor sports arenas, local buses, trams and the Metro. But smokers have their way in intercity buses and trains.

A packet of cigarettes/matches.	**Um maço de cigarros/fósforos.**
filter-tipped	**filtro**
without filter	**sem filtro**

CLOTHING (*roupa*). Unless you come to Lisbon in an unseasonably cold winter you'll never really have to dress warmly. Most Lisboans have never seen snow; only once or twice a year, as a rule, does the temperature dip below the freezing point. Spring and fall are relatively balmy, so you probably won't need anything heavier than a sweater.

Summer days can be quite hot, but pack a light wrap for the occasional unusually cool evening.

As for formality, Lisbon has changed drastically. Now virtually no establishment requires a tie. The Estoril Casino "recommends" but does not insist that men wear jackets in the evenings; yet women often wear long dresses.

When buying shoes or clothing, the following conversion table should be useful:

Men						
Clothing		Shirts		Shoes		
GB/USA	Port.	GB/USA	Port.	GB	USA	Port.
35	36	14	35	6	6½	39
36	38	15	38	7	7½	40
37	40	16	41	7½	8	41
38	42	17	43	8	8½	42
39	44	17 ¼	44	9	9½	43
40	46			10	10½	44

Women								
Clothing			Shirts/Pullovers			Shoes		
GB	USA	Port.	GB	USA	Po.	GB	USA	Port.
10	8	38	32	10	38	3	4½	35½
12	10	40	34	12	40	4	5½	36½
14	12	42	36	14	42	5	6½	37½
16	14	44	38	16	44	6	7½	38½
18	16	46	40	18	46	6½	8	39
20	18	48	42	20	48	7	8½	39½

Will I need a tie?   **É preciso gravata?**
Is it all right if I wear this?   **Vou bem assim?**

COMPLAINTS (reclamação). All complaints about over-charging or bad service should be made to the management of the shop, hotel or restaurant concerned, or directly to the head office of the department of tourism at Av. António Augusto de Aguiar 86, 1100-Lisboa, tel. 57 52 86. You should bring documents along to support your claim where possible.

CONSULATES and EMBASSIES *(consulado; embaixada)*

Australia—Embassy: Av. da Liberdade 244, 4°, tel. 53 91 08.

Canada—Embassy/Consulate: Rua Rosa Araújo 2, 6°, tel. 56 25 47.

Eire—Embassy/Consulate: Rua S. Bernardo 9, 1°-D, tel. 66 15 69.

South Africa—Embassy: Av Luís Bivar 10/10 A, tel. 53 50 41.

United Kingdom—Embassy: Rua S. Domingos-Lapa 37, tel. 66 11 91.

U.S.A.—Embassy: Av. Duque de Loulé 39, tel. 57 01 02. Consulate: Av. Duque de Loulé 47, 6°-D, tel. 57 01 02.

Most embassies and consulates are open Monday to Friday, from 9 or 10 a.m. with a 1 to 2½ hour break in the middle of the day.

Where's the British/American embassy?
It's very urgent.

Onde é a embaixada inglesa/americana?
É muito urgente.

CONVERTER CHARTS. For fluid and distance measures, see page 111. Portugal uses the metric system.

Temperature

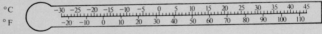

Length

Weight

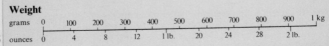

CREDIT CARDS (*cartão de crédito*). Standard international credit cards are accepted in major hotels, restaurants and tourist-oriented enterprises as well as car rental agencies. But if you're touring in the hinterland don't expect to be able to use a credit card.

Can I pay with this credit card?   **Posso pagar com cartão de crédito?**

CRIME and THEFT (*delito; roubo*). It's always wise to keep your valuables in the hotel safe. Report any theft to the hotel receptionist, the nearest police station or the local tourist office. Bag-snatching has become more frequent, so carry your handbag firmly under your arm, on the side away from the street. Pickpockets abound in the streets and especially in cafés in the Rossio Square and other spots frequented by tourists.

I want to report a theft.   **Quero participar um roubo.**

CURRENCY (*moeda*). Don't be appalled when you see price tags quoting many digits punctuated by the $ sign. Here it means *escudo* (abbreviated *esc.*), not dollar; the sign normally replaces the decimal point (thus 5.000 $ 00 means 5,000 escudos). The escudo is divided into 100 *centavos*. Coins of 10 and 20 centavos rarely come a tourist's way, but the 50-centavo coin (*cinco tostões* in slang) is common along with 1-, $2^{1}/_{2}$- and 5-escudo coins. There is also a rare 10-escudo and a new 25-escudo coin. Banknotes come in denominations of 20, 50, 100, 500 and 1,000 escudos (equalling one *conto*). For currency restrictions, see CUSTOMS CONTROLS.

CURRENCY EXCHANGE—see **BANKS**

CUSTOMS CONTROLS (*alfândega*). When you arrive at the airport go through the green channel if you have nothing to declare, the red one if you do. Here's what you can take into Portugal duty-free and, upon your return home, into your own country:

C

Into:	Cigarettes	Cigars		Tobacco	Spirits		Wine
Portugal	200	or	50	or 250 g.	1 l.	and	2 l.
Australia	200	or	250 g. or	250 g.	1 l.	or	1 l.
Canada	200	and	50	and 900 g.	1.1 l.	or	1.1 l.
Eire	200	or	50	or 250 g.	1 l.	and	2 l.
N. Zealand	200	or	50	or ½ lb.	1 qt.	and	1 qt.
S. Africa	400	and	50	and 250 g.	1 l.	and	1 l.
U.K.	200	or	50	or 250 g.	1 l.	and	2 l.
U.S.A.	200	and	100	and *	1 l.	or	1 l.

* A reasonable quantity.

In addition to personal clothing, jewellery and a small quantity of perfume, you are also allowed to take in a camera with two rolls of film, a cine (movie) camera with two rolls of film, a pair of binoculars, a portable radio and other items of a personal nature.

On departure you can buy spirits and tobacco at the airport's duty-free shop.

Currency restrictions: Tourists from abroad may take in or out of the country no more than 5,000 escudos in Portuguese currency. The amount of foreign currency you may take in either direction is unlimited, though you must declare anything over the equivalent of 30,000 escudos upon arrival.

I've nothing to declare.	**Não tenho nada a declarar.**
It's for my personal use.	**É para uso pessoal.**

D   **DRIVING IN PORTUGAL.** If you're driving to Portugal, you need only your national driving licence, the car registration papers and (although not obligatory, highly recommended) insurance coverage. The usual formula is the Green Card, an extension to the normal policy which makes it valid in other countries.

Driving conditions: The rules of the road are the same as in other European countries. You must wear seat-belts when driving outside the cities. In the towns, pedestrians have priority at zebra-crossings—but if you're on foot, don't bank on it!

Speed limits: Normally the only limit on highways is common sense, but restrictions are imposed for holiday weekends and other dangerous periods: 120 kilometres per hour (k.p.h.) on motorways and 90 on highways. In towns the limit is 60 k.p.h. unless otherwise marked. On the suspension bridge across the Tagus, the Ponte 25 de Abril, 60 k.p.h. is the maximum, 40 the minimum allowed.

Parking regulations: Unless there's an indication to the contrary, you can park as long as you wish. If marked, a sign will specify the maximum time you can stay. Car-parks and garages are also available.

Fluid measures

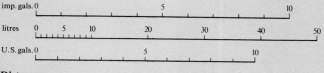

Distance

Repairs: If you belong to a motoring organization affiliated with the Automóvel Clube de Portugal you can make use of their emergency and repair services free of charge. Otherwise, most garages in Portugal are equipped to handle the usual problems. See EMERGENCIES.

Road signs: The standard international picture-signs are used in Portugal, but you'll encounter some written notices as well. Among those most frequently seen are:

Alto	Halt
Cruzamento	Crossroads
Curva perigosa	Dangerous bend (curve)
Descida ingreme	Steep hill
Desvio	Diversion (detour)
Encruzilhada	Crossroads
Estacionamento permitido	Parking allowed
Estacionamento proíbido	No parking
Guiar com cuidado	Drive with care
Obras	Road works (men working)
Paragem de autocarro	Bus stop
Pare	Stop

D

Passagem proibida	No entry
Pedestres, peões	Pedestrians
Perigo	Danger
Posto de socorros	First-aid post
Proibida a entrada	No entry
Saída de camiões	Lorry (truck) exit
Seguir pela direita/esquerda	Keep right/left
Sem saída	No through road
Sentido proíbido	No entry
Sentido único	One-way street
Silêncio	Silence zone
Stop	Stop
Trabalhos	Road works (men working)
Trânsito proíbido	No through traffic
Veículos pesados	Heavy vehicles
Velocidade máxima	Maximum speed

Are we on the right road for...?	É esta a estrada para...?
Fill the tank, please, super.	Encha o depósito de super, por favor.
Check the oil/tires/battery.	Verifique o óleo/os pneus/a bateria, se faz favor.
I've had a breakdown.	O meu carro está avariado.
There's been an accident.	Houve um acidente.

DRUGSTORES—see MEDICAL CARE

DRY CLEANING—see LAUNDRY

E

ELECTRIC CURRENT *(corrente eléctrica)*. Everywhere in Portugal the standard is 220-volt, 50-cycle A.C. For American appliances, transformers and plug adaptors are needed.

I need an adaptor/a battery, please.	Preciso de um adaptador/uma pilha, por favor.

EMBASSIES—see CONSULATES

EMERGENCIES *(urgência)*. The following numbers are useful 24 hours a day in case of emergency:

Police	115
Fire	32 22 22
Ambulance (Red Cross)	66 53 42
British Hospital	60 20 20

For emergency road service if you have a breakdown there's a 24-hour service at 77 54 75; ask for *pronto socorro*. English-speaking personnel are available between 9.30 a.m. and midnight. See also DRIVING.

Although you can call the police from any one of the blue boxes in the street marked *polícia*, it's unlikely you'll get anyone on the other end who speaks anything but Portuguese.

For emergency dental care, the hospital of São José, Rua José Antonio Serrano, tel. 86 01 31, has 24-hour general emergency service which includes dental treatment. See also MEDICAL CARE.

ENTRY FORMALITIES. See also CUSTOMS CONTROLS and DRIVING. American, British, Canadian and Irish citizens need only a valid passport—no visa—to visit Portugal, and even this requirement is waived for the British who may enter on the simplified Visitor's Passport. Though Europeans and North American residents aren't subject to any health requirements, visitors from farther afield may need a smallpox vaccination certificate. Check with your travel agent before departure.

Within 48 hours of arrival, every visitor must register with the police. In practice, this is done by your hotel receptionist who fills out a card for you to sign. But if you're staying in an apartment or villa, remember to check in at the local police station.

The length of stay authorized for tourists is 60 days (90 for Australians).

FERRIES. The two main ferry stations are next to each other: the Sul e Sueste (the larger building) and the Alfândega quay. The first serves only Seixal and Barreiro, where you catch south-bound trains (see also TRAINS).

From the Alfândega quay ferries run to Cacilhas/Almada and Montijo. You can also catch the Cacilhas/Almada ferry at the Cais do Sodré ferry station near the railway station of the same name. At Belém you can get a ferry to Trafaria or Porto Brandão which leaves from the Transtejo E.P. station (you buy tickets on the boat).

From July to September, there are four ferry crossings a day between Sesimbra, Setúbal and the peninsula of Tróia, and hovercraft services connect Tróia and Setúbal at frequent intervals.

G **GUIDES**. Arrangements may be made through the tourist office. All guides must belong to the professional association of guides and meet their standards. A guide or interpreter can be hired directly through their association in Lisbon at Rua do Telhal 4, 3°, tel. 36 71 70 from 9 a.m. to 1 p.m. and from 2.30 to 6 p.m.

For guided tours you should check with the tourist office or a travel agent for information on half- or full-day city tours.

We'd like an English-speaking guide.	**Queremos um guia que fale inglês.**

H **HAIRDRESSERS** *(cabeleireiros)*; **BARBERS** *(barbeiros)*. As in any city, typical prices are far less in neighbourhood salons than in the most chic establishments. You should tip the hairdresser about 10 per cent.

The following expressions might be useful:

haircut	**corte**
blow-dry (brushing)	**brushing**
permanent wave	**permanente**
a colour chart	**um mostruário de cores**
a colour rinse	**uma rinsage**
manicure	**manicura**
shampoo and set	**lavar e mise**
razor cut	**corte à navalha**
shave	**barba**
Not too much off (here).	**Não corte muito (aqui).**
A little more off (here).	**Corte mais um pouco (aqui).**

HITCH-HIKING. Apart from motorways (expressways), where it's forbidden, thumbing your way around should pose no big problems, and is increasingly common in Portugal.

Can you give us a lift to…?	**Pode levar-nos a…?**

HOURS *(horas de abertura)*. Principal opening hours for shops and offices are from 9 a.m. to 1 p.m. and 3 to 7 p.m. weekdays, and from 9 a.m. to 1 p.m. Saturdays. Museums are closed on Mondays and holidays. On every other day (including Sunday) they are open from 11 a.m. until 5 p.m. See also BANKS.

HOTELS and ACCOMMODATION. Hotels throughout Portugal are officially inspected and classified with one to five stars. The rates are lower in a less elaborate sort of hostelry—an *estalagem* or inn, or a *pensão* where room and board are available. Luxury-class hotels have their own nightclubs, restaurants, swimming pools, saunas, etc., but on the other end of the scale you can have a double room with bath in a *pensão* for a fraction of the cost!

Pousadas (similar to the Spanish *paradores*) are state-run establishments installed in scenic castles, palaces, convents and other historical sites, or built in out-of-the-way places to acquaint tourists with traditions in different parts of the country. Special attention is given to local food and wine as well as to the architecture and handicrafts of the region. Ask for the detailed brochure listing these at the tourist office.

When you arrive at your hotel, inn or other, you'll receive a form which sets out the conditions, prices and room number. Continental breakfast is included in the cost of a room. You'll find some typical rates listed on page 103. See also YOUTH HOSTELS.

a double/single room with/ without bath	**um quarto duplo/simples com/ sem banho**
What's the rate per night?	**Qual o preço por noite?**

LANGUAGE. Portuguese, a derivative of Latin, is at home in such diverse spots as Brazil and Macao. Your high-school Spanish may help you with signs and menus but will not unlock the mysteries of spoken Portuguese. Almost all Portuguese understand Spanish. Portuguese children study French from the age of 10 and English from 13.

The Berlitz phrasebook PORTUGUESE FOR TRAVELLERS covers practically all the situations you're likely to encounter during a visit to Portugal. Here are a few words to get you going:

Good morning	**Bom dia** (pron. bawng **dee**er)
Good evening	**Boa noite** (pron. boaer **nawng**ter)
Thank you	**Obrigado** (women say **obrigada**)
Please	**Por favor** (pron. poor fer**voar**)
Good-bye	**Adeus** (pron. erdheh**oosh**)
Yes	**Sim** (pron. seeng)
No	**Não** (pron. nahng)
Does anyone speak English?	**Alguém fala inglês?**
I don't speak Portuguese.	**Não falo português.**

LAUNDRY and DRY CLEANING *(lavandaria; tinturaria)*. There are self-service laundries in and around Lisbon; you can find them listed under "lavandarias e tinturarias" in the yellow pages phone book. Their hours are limited (9 a.m. to 1 p.m., 3 to 7 p.m. weekdays, 9 a.m. to noon on Saturdays) and none are right in the centre of Lisbon.

Most dry cleaners take three or four days, although one in the Rossio station shopping centre will do urgent work for the next day.

When will it be ready?	**Quando estará pronto?**
I must have this for tomorrow morning.	**Preciso disto para amanhã de manhã.**

LOST PROPERTY *(objectos perdidos)*. The police have a special lost property office at Rua dos Anjos 56, tel. 36 61 41. If you've lost something in a Lisbon bus or tram, go to the public transport lost-and-found department at the base of the Santa Justa lift near the Rossio station.

I've lost my wallet/purse/passport.	**Perdi a minha carteira/mala/passaporte.**

MAIL. If you don't know where you'll be staying you can have mail sent to you poste restante (general delivery) in any town. In Lisbon the most convenient way would be to specify the central branch, thus:

> Ms. Jane Jones
> Posta Restante
> Praça dos Restauradores 58
> 1200-Lisboa, Portugal

Take your passport to pick up mail at the *posta restante* window. You will be charged a small handling fee for each letter received.

Have you received any mail for…?	**Tem correio para…?**

MAPS. The tourist office has free pamphlets in English which contain maps of Lisbon and vicinity. Bookstores and news-stands sell more detailed maps by domestic and foreign publishers, including one by Falk-Verlag of Hamburg, which prepared the maps in this guide. The Automóvel Clube de Portugal has recently issued a most comprehensive street map of the city.

a street map of Lisbon	**uma planta de Lisboa**
a road map of Portugal	**um mapa das estradas de Portugal**

MEDICAL CARE. See also EMERGENCIES. Medical insurance to cover the risk of illness or accident while abroad is a worthwhile investment. Your travel agent or regular insurance company will have modestly priced policies available.

Farmácias (chemists' shops; drugstores) are open during normal business hours. At other times one shop in each neighbourhood is always on duty round the clock. Addresses are listed in the newspapers and on the door of every other chemist's shop.

a doctor	**um médico**
a dentist	**um dentista**
an ambulance	**uma ambulância**
hospital	**hospital**
an upset stomach	**mal de estômago**
sunstroke	**uma insolação**
a fever	**febre**

MEETING PEOPLE. A certain amount of formality seems inevitable in a country where people address strangers in the third person. "How are you" and "How is she/he?" are the same in Portuguese. But though reserved, the Portuguese are certainly most hospitable. And young people, as everywhere, are more spontaneous and outgoing.

The Portuguese shake hands at every opportunity. But don't be startled if somebody taps you firmly on the arm to attract your attention. It's the Portuguese way. And if people, especially villagers, seem to be staring at you, it's only unaffected curiosity.

One problem of protocol is how to catch the eye of a waiter. The Portuguese have no equivalent for "Waiter!" but use the term *Faz favor* (please!). See also LANGUAGE.

METRO—see **PUBLIC TRANSPORT**

NEWSPAPERS and MAGAZINES *(jornal; revista)*. Europe's principal newspapers, including most British dailies and the *International Herald Tribune*, edited in Paris, are regularly available on the day of publication at many newsagents and hotels. Popular foreign magazines are also sold at the same shops or stands. For cinema and theatre programmes, check one of the local Portuguese-language dailies; the most complete listings are in *Diário de Notícias*.

Have you any English-language newspapers?	**Tem jornais em inglês?**

P

PHOTOGRAPHY *(fotografia)*. Well-known brands of film in all sizes are sold at photo shops and hotel news-stands. Certain black-and-white or colour film is processed in two to three days; others take longer because they are sent out of Portugal for processing.

Aside from possible military secrets, there are no restrictions on what you may film.

Photo shops sell lead-coated plastic bags that protect films from x-rays at airport security checkpoints—or you can keep films separate from your luggage and pass them across the counter at the checkpoint to avoid possible damage.

I'd like a film for this camera.	**Quero um rolo para esta máquina.**
a black-and-white film	**um rolo a preto e branco**
a colour film	**um rolo a cores**
a colour-slide film	**um rolo de diapositivos a cores**
35-mm film	**um rolo de trinta e cinco milímetros**
super-8	**super oito**
How long will it take to develop this film?	**Quanto tempo leva a revelar este filme?**
May I take a picture?	**Posso tirar uma fotografia?**

POLICE *(polícia)*. The national police, wearing grey uniforms and armed with pistols, maintain public order and oversee Lisbon traffic. Policemen assigned to traffic duty wear red armbands with a silver letter "T" on a red background. Directing the flow of cars they wear white helmet and white gloves. On highways, traffic is controlled by the Guarda Nacional Republicana in white cars or on motorcycles. Occasionally they make spot-checks on documents or the condition of tires. The way to address any policeman is "Senhor Guarda".

Where's the nearest police station?	**Onde fica o posto de polícia mais próximo?**

POST OFFICE *(correios)*. Mail service is quite efficient in Lisbon, where a post office convenient for tourists is open 24 hours a day (see below). Most mailboxes on the street follow the British pillar-box design; they're painted bright red, too.

Local post offices are open from 9 a.m. to 7 p.m., Monday to Friday. Major branch offices also operate on Saturday mornings till noon. Round-the-clock service for the public may be found at the airport and in the big branch office in Praça dos Restauradores (opposite the tourist office). You can buy stamps from tobacconists' as well as at post offices. See also MAIL.

Telegrams: Post offices handle long-distance telephone, telegraph and telex traffic. The Marconi Company, with headquarters in Praça Marquês de Pombal, operates a private service of international communications.

I want to send a telegram to...	**Quero mandar um telegrama para...**
A stamp for this letter/postcard, please.	**Um selo para esta carta/este postal, por favor.**
express (special delivery)	**expresso**
airmail	**via aérea**
registered	**registado**
poste restante (general delivery)	**posta restante**

PRICES. Except for cars and the fuel to keep them running, things aren't notably expensive in Portugal compared to European or American prices. Of course, everything is less in non-tourist establishments. Certain rates are listed on page 103 to give you an idea of what things cost.

Is there an admission charge?	**Paga-se entrada?**
How much, please?	**Quanto é, se faz favor?**

PUBLIC HOLIDAYS (*feriado*)

Jan. 1	*Ano Novo*	New Year's Day
April 25	*Dia de Portugal*	National Day
May 1	*Dia do Trabalho*	Labour Day
June 10	*Dia de Camões*	Camoens' Day
Aug. 15	*Assunção*	Assumption
Oct. 5	*Dia da República*	Republic Day
Nov. 1	*Todos-os-Santos*	All Saints' Day
Dec. 1	*Restauração*	Restoration Day (of Independence)
Dec. 8	*Imaculada Conceição*	Immaculate Conception
Dec. 25	*Natal*	Christmas Day
Movable dates:	*Sexta-feira Santa*	Good Friday
	Corpo de Deus	Corpus Christi

These are only the national holidays of Portugal. Many special holidays affect different branches of the economy or regions of the country. Lisbon, for instance, has a local holiday—June 13—in honour of St. Anthony.

Are you open tomorrow?   **Estão abertos amanhã?**

PUBLIC TRANSPORT. See also TRAINS. You'll see more of Lisbon from the top of a green double-decker bus than from the back seat of a taxi. Or take a tram—the last word in local colour—or the underground (subway) system which is modern and fast. Most public transport operates from 6 or 7 a.m. until midnight or 1 a.m. Rates are given on page 103.

Buses: All bus stops have signs indicating the numbers of buses which stop there. You can get a free map of the entire transit system at information posts of Carris (literally "rails"), the local transport authority. The main one is at the base of the Santa Justa lift, near the Rossio station. Some buses load from the front, others from the rear so you'll just have to follow the crowd. There may be a conductor just inside the door who'll check your pass, or sell you the appropriate ticket. Otherwise, take a seat and the collector will come to you. Keep your ticket for the whole trip in case an inspector boards the bus to double-check.

Inter-city buses: There are a number of terminals in Lisbon which serve different parts of the country. It's easier for a tourist to ask where the bus leaves from at the tourist office in Praça dos Restauradores. Buses are good and prices are reasonable; you tend to see more of the country than if you go by train. Two sample journeys: Lisbon to Castelo Branco, 256 kilometres, takes about 4 hours; Lisbon to Coimbra, 200 kilometres, takes $3^1/_2$ hours.

Trams: They may be rickety and slow but you can't deny that these yellow veterans throb with nostalgia. At last count over 40 of the trolleycars in daily operation in Lisbon had been built before the First World War! Tram stops are marked by large signs saying *Paragem* (stop), often hanging from the wires above the street. The Carris bus map shows all tram routes as well. Board through the rear door—a conductor will sell you a ticket at the door or once you're seated. On **funiculars** you'll always pay at the door.

Metro: Lisbon's underground railway system, the Metropolitano, or Metro, has only 20 stations, most of which are in residential districts of scant interest to tourists. Charts of the route system are posted in every station and carriage. A complication is that several stations have short platforms at which only the fore or aft two cars of a four-car train open their doors. The worst that can happen is that you're locked in until the next stop. To avoid this, check the map carefully and then follow the directions, in several languages, posted on the platform before you board the train.

Fares: You can buy a tourist pass good for 7 days which is valid on trams, buses and funiculars—but not on the Metro—within the main transport zone of Lisbon. For the Metro there is a book of ten tickets *(caderneta)* available at the ticket window.

How much is the fare to…?	**Quanto custa o bilhete para…?**
Will you tell me when to get off?	**Pode dizer-me quando devo descer?**
Where's the nearest bus/tram stop?	**Onde fica a mais próxima paragem dos autocarros/eléctricos?**

RADIO and TV *(rádio; televisão).* Two government-operated television channels serve Portugal. Feature films are usually shown in the original language with subtitles.

The government operates four radio channels. Programme Two consists amost entirely of classical music, Programme Four of almost uninterrupted pop music. The only non-government radio station is Radio Renascença, a commercial station owned by the Catholic Church.

Travel suggestions in English for tourists are broadcast every morning on Programme Two (755 khz medium wave, 94.3 mhz FM) at 8.15 a.m.

Shortwave programmes of the Voice of America, BBC, Radio Canada International and other foreign stations can be picked up clearly at certain times of day, usually early morning and night.

RELIGIOUS SERVICES *(serviço religioso).* Most Portuguese are Roman Catholic. For English-speaking Catholics mass is held on Sundays at the Dominican Church of Corpo Santo, Travessa do Corpo Santo 32, Lisbon, tel. 32 32 08.

Anglican services are conducted in English on Sundays at St. George's Church, Rua da Estrela 4, tel. 66 30 10, in the Estrela district of Lisbon. **121**

R   Church of Scotland (Presbyterian) services are held on Sundays at Rua da Arriaga 11, tel. 66 30 10.

The Shaare Tikva Synagogue is located at Rua Alexandre Herculano 59, tel. 65 86 04.

What time is mass/the service?	**A que horas é a missa/o culto?**
Is it in English?	**É em inglês?**

S   **SHOESHINES** *(engraxador)*. Most hotels will shine your shoes if you leave them outside your bedroom door at night. Shoeshine men will find you in a café if your shoes are a bit dusty, or you can patronize any of the small shoeshine shops.

T   **TAXIS** *(táxi)*. Lisbon taxis are black with a green roof and a sign reading *taxi*. In rural areas similar cars marked "A" (meaning *aluguer*— for hire) perform the taxi function but without meters. Every neighbourhood has a taxi rank; you can also find them at railway, Metro and ferry stations.

The fare is shown on the meter. There is no extra charge for night work, but drivers add 50 per cent to the meter charge if you have more than 30 kilogrammes (66 pounds) of baggage. A tip of 10 to 15 per cent would be appropriate.

Where can I get a taxi?	**Onde posso encontrar um táxi?**
Taxi!	**Táxi!**
What's the fare to...?	**Quanto custa o percurso até...?**

TELEGRAMS—see **POST OFFICE**

TELEPHONES *(telefone)*. Automatic street telephones are usually found in British-style phone boxes (booths). You deposit several of the coins necessary; unused ones will be returned.

From Lisbon you can dial direct to Great Britain and other European countries.

For international operator-connected calls from Lisbon (e.g. to U.S.A., Canada, Australia or New Zealand) dial the English-speaking operator at 32 90 11.

Numbers for overseas operator-connected calls *outside* Lisbon are all different; if possible, you should have the hotel receptionist book your call. Or ask for instructions from the English-speaking operator at 17.

reverse-charge call	**paga pelo destinatário**
person-to-person call	**com préaviso**
Can you get me this number in…?	**Pode ligar-me para este número em…?**

TIME DIFFERENCES. In winter Portugal runs on Greenwich Mean Time (GMT). From the first Sunday in April to the first Sunday in October the clocks are moved one hour ahead to summer time. In summer the chart looks like this:

Sydney	Auckland	New York	**Lisbon**	London
9 p.m.	11 p.m.	7 a.m.	**noon**	noon

What time is it, please? **Que horas são, por favor?**

TOILETS *(retretes).* Public conveniences are located in most Metro stations and other heavily-travelled places in Lisbon. If there's an attendant on duty, a 5-escudo coin would be an appropriate tip. "Ladies" is *Senhoras* and "Gentlemen", *Homens.*

Where are the toilets? **Onde ficam os toilets?**

TOURIST INFORMATION. The Portuguese government maintains tourist offices in more than a dozen foreign cities. Here are some useful addresses:

British Isles: Portuguese National Tourist Office, New Bond Street House, 1, New Bond St., London W1; tel.: (01) 493-3873

Canada: Portuguese National Tourist Office, 390 Bay St., Toronto, Ont. M5H 2Y2; tel.: (416) 364-8133

U.S.A.: Portuguese National Tourist Office, 548 Fifth Ave., New York 10036; tel.: (212) 354-4403

Suite 500, Palmer House, 17 E. Monroe St. Chicago IL. 60603; tel.: (312) 236-6603

Suite 1305, 1 Park Plaza, 3250 Wilshire Blvd., Los Angeles, CA 90010; tel.: (213) 380-6459

In Lisbon, the national tourist office (Direcção-Geral do Turismo) is located in the Palácio Foz, Praça dos Restauradores, tel. 366307. Multilingual personnel answer questions, offer advice and provide maps and brochures. Smaller offices may be found at key tourist spots in Lisbon and in Estoril, Sintra and Setúbal.

T

The Lisbon tourist office (Posto de Turismo da Camara Municipal de Lisboa) is on Rua Jardim do Regedor, tel. 36 95 64. There is a special number for information in English: 36 94 50.

Where's the tourist office?   **Onde fica o turismo?**

TRAINS (*comboio*). Lisbon has four principal railway stations scattered around the city. International services and trains for northern Portugal originate at Santa Apolónia station. It's easy to reach this main station by bus—you take the 9 or 9a in the Avenida da Liberdade. Commuter trains for the western suburbs and Estoril and Cascais leave from Cais do Sodré. Trains for Sintra and the west depart from Rossio station. And the fourth busy station, called Sul e Sueste (South and South-east) has ferryboats which cross the Tagus to meet the trains that go on as far as the Algarve. The price of the ticket includes the ferry link. See also FERRIES.

In the major stations first- and second-class tickets are sold at separate windows. A first-class carriage usually has a yellow stripe above the windows and the number "1" near the doors.

When does the train for... leave?   **Quando parte o comboio para...?**

single (one-way)   **ida**
return (round-trip)   **ida e volta**

TRAVELLER'S CHEQUES—see **BANKS**

W

WATER. Although Lisbon's tap water tastes heavily of chemicals, it's safe for drinking. You can buy bottled drinking water—Portugal has an excellent range of local mineral waters.

a bottle of mineral water   **uma garrafa de água mineral**
carbonated/non-carbonated   **com/sem gás**

Y

YOUTH HOSTELS (*pousadas de juventude*). Young tourists from 14 up can stay in dormitories at very low rates if they're members of a national or international youth hostel association. Membership in the Portuguese Youth Hostel Association is open to "juniors" (aged 14 to 21) and "seniors" (22 to 40). Parents with children younger than 14 may, in certain cases, stay in these hostels if there is room, but preference is given to those within the set age brackets. You can get in touch with the Associação Portuguesa de Pousadas de Juventude at Rua Andrade Corvo 46, 1000-Lisboa, tel. 57 10 54.

SOME USEFUL EXPRESSIONS

yes/no	**sim/não**
please/thank you	**por favor/obrigado (obrigada)**
excuse me/you're welcome	**perdão/de nada**
where/when/how	**onde/quando/como**
how long/how far	**quanto tempo/a que distância**
yesterday/today/tomorrow	**ontem/hoje/amanhã**
day/week/month/year	**dia/semana/mês/ano**
left/right	**esquerdo/direito**
good/bad	**bom/mau**
big/small	**grande/pequeno**
cheap/expensive	**barato/caro**
hot/cold	**quente/frio**
old/new	**velho/novo**
open/closed	**aberto/fechado**

Does anyone here speak English?	**Alguém fala inglês?**
I don't understand.	**Não compreendo.**
Please write it down.	**Escreva-mo, por favor.**
What does this mean?	**Que quer dizer isto?**
Help me, please.	**Ajude-me, por favor.**
Get a doctor quickly.	**Chame um médico, depressa.**
What time is it?	**Que horas são?**
How much is that?	**Quanto custa isto?**
I'd like…	**Queria/Quero…**
Just a minute.	**Um momento.**
Waiter!/Waitress!	**Faz favor!**

DAYS

Sunday	**domingo**	Thursday	**quinta-feira**
Monday	**segunda-feira**	Friday	**sexta-feira**
Tuesday	**terça-feira**	Saturday	**sábado**
Wednesday	**quarta-feira**		

What day is it today?	**Que dia é hoje?**

Index

An asterisk (*) next to a page number indicates a map reference. For museums, churches, etc. outside Lisbon, see under individual towns.

INDEX